A SENIORS GUIDE TO THE S23 AND S23 ULTRA

AN EASV TO UNDERSTAND GUIDE TO THE
2023 SAMSUNG S SERIES PHONE

SCOTT LA COUNTE

RIDICULOUSLY
SIMPLE BOOKS

ANAHEIM, CALIFORNIA

www.RidiculouslySimpleBooks.com

Disclaimer: *Please note, while every effort has been made to ensure accuracy, this book is not endorsed by Samsung, Inc. and should be considered unofficial.*

Table of Contents

INTRODUCTION

Looking for a guide that will help you get the most out of your new Samsung Galaxy S23 without overwhelming you with irrelevant information? Look no further than this concise and user-friendly book!

With a focus on the most popular features, this guide is perfect for those who want to quickly and easily learn how to make the most of their phone. Inside, you'll find step-by-step instructions on everything from setting up your phone to using the camera, surfing the internet, and changing system settings.

But that's not all! You'll also learn what makes Galaxy different from other smartphones, how to use Samsung SmartTag, and about the accessibility features that make the phone accessible to everyone.

So if you're looking for a practical and easy-to-follow guide to mastering the S23's most powerful features, look no further than this book!

Inside, you'll learn about:
- What makes Galaxy different from iOS, Android, and other smartphones
- Using Samsung SmartTag

- Setting up your phone
- Making calls
- Installing apps
- Accessibility features
- Using the camera
- Surfing the Internet
- Changing system settings
- And much more!

As a bonus, this guide includes a comprehensive guide on using Google Search, ensuring that you have everything you need to get up and running quickly.

NOTE: This guide is not endorsed by Samsung and should be considered unofficial.

[1]
Start Here

S22 VS S23

I know you are eager to get into how to use the phone, but before we get there, let's pause and talk about how the S23 is different from other phones. I'll start by talking about how the S23 is different (and similar) to the S22.

Looking at the S22 and S23 side by side, you'll notice that they're pretty similar. Turn them on, and the similarities don't stop. Both, after all, run the same One UI 5.1 software. So why are people upgrading? The details can be hard to notice at first, but they are still important.

Both devices support 5G, but the S23 has a more advance network technology that can help it browse the Internet faster in some situations.

Many users probably won't notice, but the display on the S23 has a slightly higher resolution.

The camera on the S23 has also made slight enhancement having a better aperture than the S22.

If battery is a concern of yours, then you'll be delighted to know the S23 has a slightly larger battery and also can charge at faster speeds.

S23 VS S23 ULTRA

Okay, so there's some improvements over the S22 with the S23; but there's also several different S23's! Three to be exactly: the S23, S23+, and S23 Ultra. What's the difference! The most obvious difference is price, but there's a lot going on with the hardware inside the device to justify the higher price points.

The S23 Ultra is the largest of all the devices, and also the strongest; while the S23 and S23 both come with a durable glass front and back with aluminum frame, the S23 takes it up a notch with a higher grade Gorilla Glass.

All of the new devices have cutting edge network technology, but the S23 ultra features the most comprehensive—including the ability to connect to Wi-Fi 6e.

Both the S23 and S23+ come with an impressive 60Hz refresh rate, but the Ultra sports stunning a

120Hz with HDR10+; on smaller screens, this high definition display might not be as impressive, but if you want the best, the Ultra is the way to go.

In terms of speed, the S23 and S23+ both have a Snapdragon 7 Gen 2 chipset; the Ultra has the faster Snapdragon 8 Gen 2 chip. The Ultra also has a Octa-core CPU.

The S23 and S23+ each have 8GB of RAM while the Ultra has 12GB of RAM; here's where some people might prefer the non-Ultra devices: they have the ability to add memory via a microSD card; that option isn't available on the Ultra.

Finally, the camera–the feature most users look to when deciding to upgrade. Both the S23 and S23+ have a triple camera setup (wide, ultra-wide, and telephoto lens) that will take amazing photos. But the Ultra takes it up a level by offering a 200 MP wide lens, and a 10 MP periscope telephoto lens. The selfie lens is 12MP on the Ultra and 10MP on the other devices. The Ultra also can shoot in 8K whereas the other phones can only do 4K; it's worth noting, however, most TVs don't support 8K, so it might be hard to find devices to show off this highest quality.

S23 VS. IPHONE 14

How do the base S23 compare to the base iPhone 14? Let's take a look.

Sitting them side by side, you'll notice that the S23 is slightly smaller and slightly lighter–the difference here is so ridiculously small that you probably will not notice.

Both device offer a HD display.

Both device also start at 128GB of storage; the S23 has 8GB of RAM whereas the iPhone has 6GB of RAM; it's worth nothing, that the memory on the S23 can be expanded with a storage card; the iPhone does not have this option.

The camera on both devices will both deliver impressive results; while the S23 does offer significantly more MP on the main lens (64 MP vs 12 MP on the iPhone), the quality of the photos is arguably very similar.

SAMSUNG S23 ULTRA VS IPHONE PRO MAX

What about the S23 Ultra against the highest quality iPhone 14 Pro Max?

Side by side, the two devices are pretty similar; the Max is a little smaller in height, but also slightly heavier (2 grams heavier).

The displays on both devices are also pretty similar; both have a 120Hz refresh rate; the Max has a slightly higher max brightness.

Both phones have a max storage of 1TB; the iPhone Pro Max starts at 128GB of storage whereas the S23 Ultra starts at 256GB. The memory on the Max is 6GB of RAM; the Ultra starts at 12GB of RAM.

But what about the main attraction: the cameras? The iPhone has a 48MP wide-angle lens, a 12 MP telephoto lens and 3X optical zoom; it also has LiDar technology; the front camera has 12MP. The Ultra has a 200 MP wide-angle camera, 10MP telephoto, a 3x and 10x optical zoom, and up to 100x digital zoom. True, the MP is much higher on the Ultra, but the quality of photos is similar on both devices.

[2]
THE OVERVIEW

This chapter will cover:
- Exploring the Samsung UI
- Notification bar
- Edge bar
- Gestures

FINDING YOUR WAY AROUND

People come to the Samsung from all sorts of different places: iPhone, other Android phone, flip phone, two Styrofoam cups tied together with string. This next section is a crash course in the interface. If you've used Android before, then it might seem a little simple, so skip ahead if you already know all of this.

If any of this seems a little rushed, there's good reason: it is! We'll cover these points in more detail later. This is just a quick starter / reference.

When you see your main screen for the first time, you will see six components. They are (from top to bottom): the Notification Bar, Add Weather Widget, Google Search App, Short Cuts Icons, Favorites Bar, navigation.

Notifications Bar - This is a pull-down menu (slide down to expand it) and it's where you'll see all your alerts (new email or text, for example) and where you can go to change settings quickly.

Add Weather Widget – Widgets are like mini apps that display information on your screen;

weather is what's shown here, but they can be anything from Gmail, to calendars, and hundreds of things in between.

Google Search App – The Google Search app is another example of a widget. As the name implies, it can search Google for information; but it also searches apps on your phone.

Short Cuts Icons – These are apps that you frequently use and want quick access to.

Favorites Bar – These are like short cuts, except you see them on all your screens. You can add whatever you want to this area, but these are the apps Samsung thinks you'll use most.

Navigation Bar – These are shortcuts for getting around your phone: the first is the multi-task button, which helps you quickly switch apps; the next is the Home button which gets you back to the Home screen; and the last is the back button, which returns you to the previous screen.

So, what are these? Real quick, these are as follows:

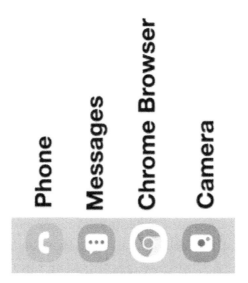

- **Phone**: Do you want to take a wild guess what the phone button does? If you said brings you an ice cream, then maybe you aren't cut out for a phone. But if you said something along the lines of "It launches an app to call people" then you'll have no problem at all with your new device. Surprise, surprise: this pricey gadget that plays games, takes pictures, and keeps you up-to-date on political ramblings on social media does one more interesting thing: it calls people!
- **Message**: Message might be a little more open-ended than "Phone"; that could mean email message, text messages,

messages you keep getting on your bathroom mirror to put the toilet seat down. In this case, it means "text messages" (but really—put that toilet seat down...you aren't doing anyone any favors). This is the app you'll use whenever you want to text cute pictures of cats.

- **Chrome**: Whenever you want to surf the Internet, you'll use Chrome. There are actually several apps that do the same thing—like Firefox and Opera—but I recommend Chrome until you are comfortable with your phone. Personally, I think it's the best app for searching the Internet, but you'll soon learn that most things on the phone are about preference, and you may find another Internet browser that suits your needs better.
- **Camera**: This apps opens pictures of vintage cameras...just kidding! It's how you take pictures on your phone. You use this same app for videos as well.

NOTIFICATIONS BAR

Next to the short cut bar, the area you'll use the most is the notification bar. This is where you'll get, you guessed it, notifications! What's a notification? That's any kind of notice you have elected to receive. A few examples: text message alerts, email alerts, amber alerts, and apps that have updates.

When you drag your finger down from the notification bar, you'll get a list of several settings that you can adjust. Press and hold any of these options and you'll open an app with even more options.

From right to left these are the options you can change or use:

- Wi-fi
- Sound (tap to mute sounds)
- Bluetooth
- Lock the device from auto-rotating
- Airplane mode (which turns off wi-fi and Bluetooth)
- Flashlight

If you continue dragging down, this thin menu expands and there are a few more options.

The first is at the bottom of the screen—it's the slider, and it makes your device brighter or dimmer depending on which way you drag it.

Above that, there are several controls. Many of these controls are just an on / off toggle, but some let you long press to see expanded options. Some will be more obvious that others, but I'll go through each one quickly, starting from top left.

- Wi-Fi – Tap to turn off Wi-Fi; long press to change networks and see Wi-Fi settings.
- Sound – Tap to turn off sound; long press to see sound settings.

- Bluetooth – Turns off Bluetooth; long press to connect to a device or see Bluetooth settings.
- Autorotate – Tapping will lock the device orientation, so if you turn the device the screen will not rotate.
- Airplane mode – turns off features like Wi-Fi, cellular, and Bluetooth.
- Flashlight – Turns on the flash of your camera to let your phone act as a flashlight.
- Mobile Data – If you want to manually control if your phone is using mobile data or Wi-Fi, then you can toggle this on. There are a lot of reasons for this; sometimes you might find the Wi-Fi connection is too weak and you want to use mobile exclusively—but be careful: depending on what you are doing, mobile data can eat up your carriers data plan very quickly.
- Mobile hotspot – Toggling this on will let your phone act as a hotspot (so other devices can use your phone's Data connection to connect to the Internet); personally, I use this often to connect to my laptop on the go. Some carriers will charge extra for this service. You should also be careful, as this does go into data charges; if you let someone else share it and they decide to stream a movie, it's

going to eat up your data quick. Long pressing it will show you expanded settings.

- Power saving mode – turns on a power saving mode that will help your phone last longer; if you are low on batteries and not near a charger, this will help you get a little more life out of your phone. Long pressing it will bring up expanded power save features.

- Location – Toggling this on / off lets apps see your location; for example, if you are using a map for driving directions, it gives the app permission to see where you are located. Long pressing will show expanded location settings.

- Link to Windows – If you have a Windows computer, you can use this feature to send notifications to your linked Windows computer.

- Screen recorder – This option lets you create a video of what's on your screen; you can create a tutorial for something or even record a game. Long pressing will show expanded settings.

If you swipe you will see even more options to pick from.

- DeX – DeX turns your phone into a desktop experience when connected to an HDMI monitor.
- Smart view – lets you mirror your screen (or sound) to other devices (such as a Google Home).
- Nearby Share – Let's you share photos and documents with phones nearby you.
- Eye comfort shield – Toggling on will turn off the blue light on your phone; it gives your phone a more brownish hue. Looking at a blue light can make it difficult to sleep, so it's recommended to turn this on at night.
- Do not disturb – Turns off notifications so you don't receive messages or phone calls (they'll go straight to voice mail); long pressing expands Do not disturb settings.
- Dark mode – Gives menus and some apps a black background instead of white. Long pressing will show expanded settings.

Samsung got rid of a lot of options that they probably felt either weren't used or weren't use that often. But they're still there. On the last notification screen, tap the + icon and you'll see more options that you can add.

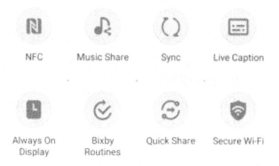

| NFC | Music Share | Sync | Live Caption |

| Always On Display | Bixby Routines | Quick Share | Secure Wi-Fi |

There are two screens of extra buttons (tap them and drag them to your notification bar to add them). The first screen shows:

- NFC – If you plan on putting credit cards on your phone to wirelessly pay for things at the checkout, make sure NFC is toggled on. Long pressing will show expanded settings.
- Music share – Shares music that you are listening to, so you can listen together. Long pressing will show expanded settings.
- Sync – Sync's your device across other devices.

- Live Captioning – This will be covered a little later, but toggling it on let's you add captions to your videos.
- Always on display – your display is always on when this is enabled. Long pressing will show expanded settings.
- Bixby routines – Sets up Bixby. Long pressing will show expanded settings.
- Quick share – This option lets you wirelessly share photos, videos and other files with another device. Long pressing will show expanded settings.
- Secure Wi-Fi – Creates a secure encryptions while using but public and personal wireless networks.

The next notification option screen has the following:

- Focus mode – Lets you set timers and turn off certain apps for a period of time to give you a more distraction-free experience. Long pressing will show expanded settings.

- Kids Home – Turns on kids mode, which gives your device a kid-friendly UI and turns off several apps.
- Enhanced Processioning – A mode that conserves battery by slowing your phone down.
- Wireless PowerShare – tapping this option lets you wirelessly power charge another wireless device (such as a watch or even another phone); your phone is essentially serving as a wireless charger to that other device. Long pressing it will bring up PowerShare settings.
- Call & text and other devices
- Secure folder – Creates a secure folder for your devices, so you can password protect certain apps and documents.
- Scan QR code – A QR code is sometimes seen on fliers; you can use this to scan it and see what the code links to.
- Dolby Amos – Toggling on will give your device superior Dolby Amos sound. Long pressing will show expanded settings.

On the notification area you'll also see two options for Media and Devices.

Media lets you control music and videos on other devices.

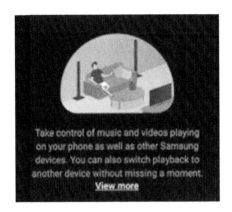

Devices lets you connect to devices using Bluetooth and see what devices you are already connected to.

Up on top is a handful of other controls.

The config button brings up expanded settings for notifications.

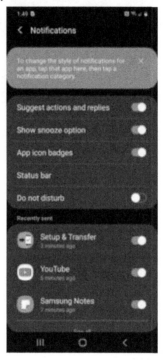

The power button will let you restart or power down your device.

GETTING AROUND QUICKLY

As mentioned, the bottom of the screen is your navigation area for getting around.

This is nice, but better is setting up gestures to handle navigating around your phone. This will turn this section off to give a tad more screen real estate.

To change it, swipe up from the bottom of your screen (this will bring up all your apps), then tap Settings. Next, go to the Display option.

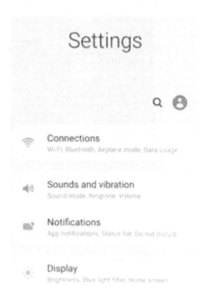

In Display options, scroll down until you get to Navigation bar, and then tap it.

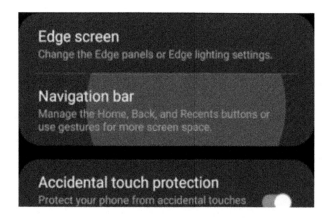

In the Navigation bar menu, select Full screen gestures.

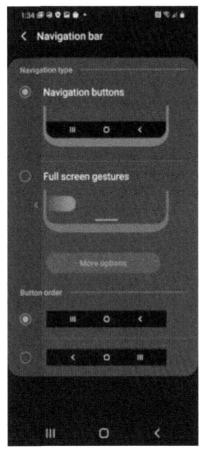

Nice! It's gone! But what are the gestures?! Before you leave settings, it will give you a little preview of how they work, but below is a recap:

- Swipe up and release to get to your Home screen from any app.
- Swipe up and hold to bring up multitasking.

- Swipe right or left from the bottom edge of your screen to go backwards and forward.

You might recall that swiping up from the bottom showed you all your apps. That gesture now returns to the Home screen, so how do you see all your apps? From your Home screen, swipe up in the middle of the screen to see them.

When it comes to getting around your Samsung, learning how to use gestures will be the quickest, most effective method. You can change some of the gesture options by going to System > Gestures > System navigation.

The most important gesture is how to get back to the Home screen—there are no buttons after all. That's the easiest one to remember: swipe up from the bottom of the screen.

MULTITASKING

Those are the easy gestures to remember; if you want to move around quickly, however, you need to know the two big multitask gestures, which help you switch between apps.

The first is to see your open apps. To do this, swipe up like you're going to the Home screen, but keep going until about the middle of the screen and then stop and lift your finger—don't make a quick swipe-up gesture like you would when going Home. This will show you previews of all of your open apps, and you can swipe between them. Tap the one you want to open.

The quickest way to switch back and forth between two or three apps, however, is to swipe from left to right along the bottom edge of the screen. This swipes between apps in the order that you have used them.

ZOOM

Need to see text bigger? There are two ways to do that. Note: this works on many, but not all apps.

The first way is to pinch to zoom.

r with the Additic
: between you an
es. It is importan
Collectively, this l
s".

etween what the
al Terms say, ther
elation to that Se

The second way is to double tap on the text.

ROTATE

You probably have noticed if you rotate your phone, it rotates the screen. What if you don't want to rotate the entire screen? You can turn that off very easily. Swipe down and then tap the "arrows" button to enable or disable it.

EDGE BAR

One of the features that has always stood out on Samsung devices is the way they make use of all areas of your phone…right up to the edge.

The Edge bar brings up short cut menus quickly no matter where you are on the phone. To access it, swipe left from the side of your screen near the top; the Edge bar outline can just barely be seen on your Home screen. It's right next to the down volume button and extends just above the up volume button.

Swiping right brings up a side menu.

On the bottom left corner, you can click the bulleted list icon to see all of your Edge bar menus.

Swiping right and left lets you toggle between them.

Clicking on the config icon on the bottom left corner will let you select and deselect the Edge bar menus that are shown.

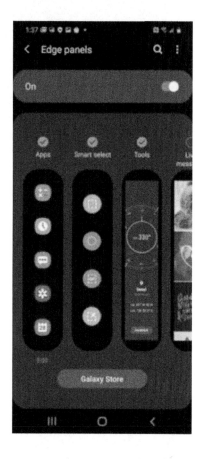

To add an app to the App Edge bar menu, just tap the + icon.

To remove an app, tap and hold the icon, then drag it to remove.

Smart select is a tool to create screenshots and GIFs (little animated images).

Rectangle captures a selected rectangle area of your screen.

You can also go to somewhere like YouTube, where this tool would automatically locate the video and record it to create a GIF. Use the GIF capture icon to do this.

The oval tool will change the capture into a circular shape.

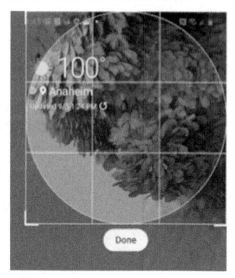

As the name implies, the Tools Edge bar, has a series of tools that you can use along with your phone. They help you take measurements, keep tallies, and use as a flashlight, or compass.

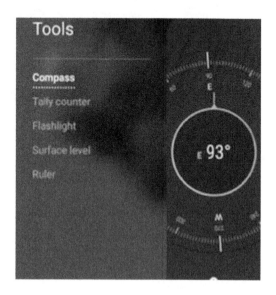

[3]
CUSTOMIZING THE PHONE

This chapter will cover:
- Customizing screens
- Split screens
- Gestures

MAKING PRETTY SCREENS

If you've used an iPhone or iPad, then you may notice the screen looks a little...bare. There are only a few buttons on it. Maybe you like that. If so, then good for you! Skip ahead. If you want to decorate that screen with shortcuts and widgets, then read on.

Adding Shortcuts

Any app you want on this screen, just find it and then press and hold; when a menu comes up, drag it upward until the screen appears and move it to where you want it to go.

To remove an app from a screen, tap and hold, then tap Remove from the pop-up box.

Widgets

Shortcuts are nice, but widgets are better. Widgets are sort of like mini-programs that run on your screen. A common widget people put on their screen is the weather forecast. Throughout the day the widget will update automatically with up-to-date info.

It's such a popular widget that Samsung has put the option on your Home screen and you only have to tap it to set it up.

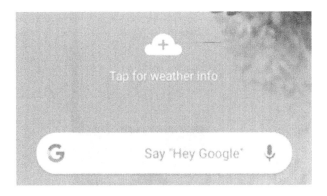

Once you add your city, it's going to automatically start showing. Clicking on it will open up the app.

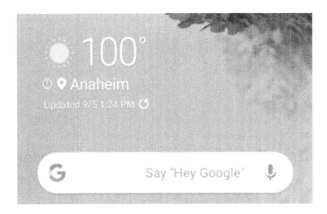

Weather is nice, but there are lots of widgets you can add to your Home screen. How do you get them?

There's actually a shortcut when you tap and hold over an app that has Widget capabilities (not all do).

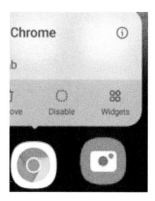

If you want to see all widgets available, then press and hold your finger on the middle of the screen. This brings up the Home screen options menu. Tap the Widgets icon.

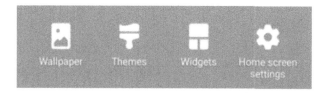

This will show you the most popular widgets, but if you know what you want, then just search for it.

For this example, I searched for Gmail, who I know has a widget. I tap it, then it let's me select where I want it on the screen.

When you tap on the widget, you'll notice little dots on the side. That lets you make it bigger or smaller. Just drag it to your ideal width and height.

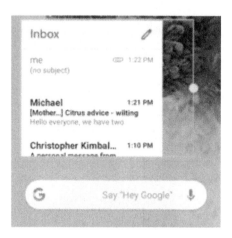

To remove any widget, just tap and hold it. From the pop-up, tap Remove from Home.

BATTERY WIDGET

If you have multiple Samsung devices (like the Galaxy Buds, S Pen, Galaxy Watch, etc), the battery widget can help you keep track of the battery life for each device.

Battery

🔲	Galaxy S23 Ultra	53%
✏️	S Pen	100%

Adding the widget is very simple:

- Tap and hold on the home screen, then select Widgets.
- Tap on the down arrow next to the Battery widget.
- You'll see two different styles: circles and list view; tap the one you want to display.
- The battery widget will now show all connected devices.
- You can go into your widget settings to change what displays and also adjust the color.

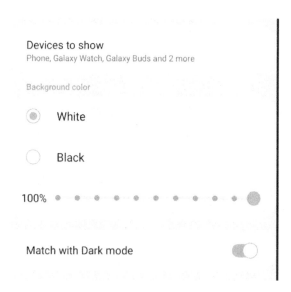

Devices to show
Phone, Galaxy Watch, Galaxy Buds and 2 more

Background color

⦿   White

◯   Black

100% ● ● ● ● ● ● ● ● ● ● ● 🔘

Match with Dark mode

WALLPAPER

Adding wallpaper to your screen is done in a similar way. Tap and hold your finger on the Home screen, when the menu comes up, select Wallpaper instead of Widgets.

From the Wallpapers menu you have a few choices:

- My wallpapers – These are wallpapers you have purchased or ones that Samsung pre-loads.
- Gallery – Pictures you've taken.
- Explore more wallpapers – Where you can buy wallpapers.
- Color palette – this let's you choose a palette of colors based on the wallpaper that you select.

Wallpapers usually cost a buck. It's not an absurd amount of money, but you can also search for custom wallpapers on the Internet that are available for free.

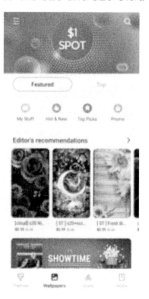

Samsung's featured wallpapers should not be overlooked. There's a lot to choose from.

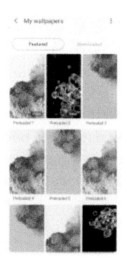

VIDEO WALLPAPER

One UI 5.1 added the ability to add video wallpaper; this only works on the lock screen—not your homescreen. You add video wallpaper the same way you do regular photos to your lock screen; the only difference is you pick a video instead.

THEMES

Picking wallpaper for your phone helps give it a bit more personality, but themes help really fine-tune the customization. You can pick icon shapes, fonts, and more.

To access them, press and hold on your Home screen, then select Themes.

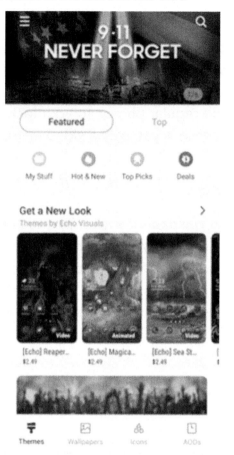

SAMSUNG FREE

Samsung Free is sort of like a recap of your day and daily recommendations for things to download. You can see it by swiping left from your Home screen.

It's not the worst feature on the phone, but a lot of people don't really see value in it. If you'd rather not see it, then tap and hold on your Home screen, then swipe left when you see the Home options. On the Samsung Daily preview, toggle the switch to off.

By default, you might have Google Discover turned on; Google Discover is the Google equivalent of Samsung Free.

ADDING SCREENS

Adding screens for even more shortcuts and widgets is easy. Tap and hold the Home screen, and swipe to the right.

Next, click the + icon which will add a screen. When you return to your Home screen, you can swipe right and start adding shortcuts and widgets to it.

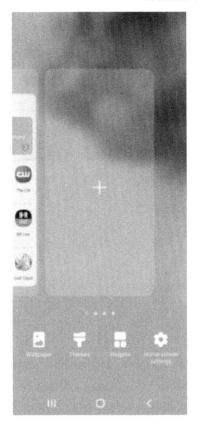

HOME SCREEN SETTINGS

To access even more Home screen settings, tap and hold the Home screen, then tap the config Home screen settings icon.

The first area that you'll probably want to change is the Home screen layout.

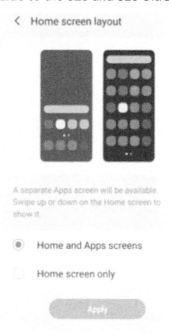

< Home screen layout

A separate Apps screen will be available.
Swipe up or down on the Home screen to
show it.

◉ Home and Apps screens

○ Home screen only

Apply

The Home screen grid is also useful if you want to get a little more use out of the screen real estate; it adjusts icon size / placement to fit more or fewer icons on the screen.

The rest of the settings are just toggle switches.

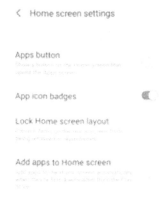

LOCK SCREEN

The lock screen is where you'll spend a lot of time; it helps you know if there's content worth unlocking your phone to see–new emails, messages, etc. But it can also start displaying too much content. If you find your lock screen is cluttered with information, then it's time to go into your settings and hide content.

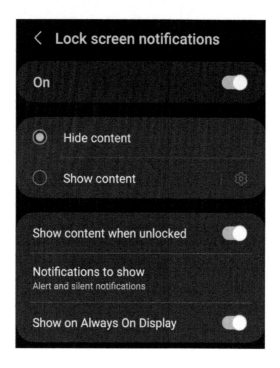

To use this feature, open your phone's settings and then go to Notifications; tap "Lock screen notification." You not will see all the options for how you want content displayed (or not displayed).

A WORD, OR TWO, ABOUT MENUS

It's pretty intuitive that if you tap on an icon, it opens the app. What's not so obvious is if you tap and hold there are other options. Every app is different. Usually, they're shortcuts—tapping and holding over the Phone icon, for example, brings up your favorites; doing the same thing over the camera brings up a selfie mode shortcut. Tap and hold over your favorite apps to see what shortcuts are available.

SPLIT SCREENS

The Samsung phone comes in different sizes; a bigger screen obviously gives you a lot more space, which makes split screen apps a pretty handy feature. It works on the smaller Samsung as well, though it doesn't feel as effective on the smaller screen.

To use this feature, swipe up to bring up multitasking; next, tap the icon above the window you want to turn into split screen (note: this feature is not supported on all apps); if split screen is available, you'll see a menu that has an option for split screen.

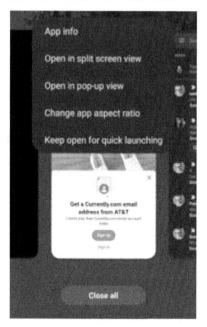

Once you tap split screen, it will let you swipe left and right to find the app you want to split the screen with. Tap the one you want.

Your screen is now split in two.

That thin blue bar in the middle is adjustable; you can move it up or down so one of the apps has more screen real estate.

To exit this mode, drag the black bar either all the way to the top or all the way to the bottom until one of the apps completely goes away.

MULTI-TASKING: POP-UP VIEW

Pop-Up View let's users drag a windows frame towards the edge of the screen to switch back to fullscreen mode.

GESTURES

Samsung has a few gestures built into the device that you can access by going into your settings app, then clicking Advanced features.

The first area to check out is Motions and gestures.

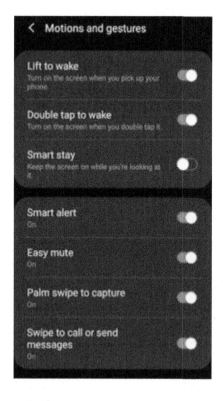

These are all toggle switches and you can see a preview of how they work by tapping on the title of the gesture.

The other setting is for One-handed mode. This is turned off by default. By toggling it on, you can see the options available to you.

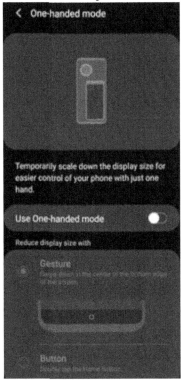

[4]

THE BASICS

This chapter will cover:
- Making calls
- Sending messages
- Finding and downloading apps
- Driving directions

Now that you have your phone set up and know your way around the device at its most basic level, let's go over the apps you'll be using the most that are currently on your shortcut or favorite bar:
- Phone
- Messages
- Chrome

Notice that Camera is off this list? There's a lot to cover with Camera, so I'll go over it in a separate chapter. In its place, I will cover the Google Play Store here, so you can begin downloading apps.

Before we get into it, there's something you need to know: how to open apps not on your favorite bar. It's easy. From your Home screen, swipe up from the middle of the screen. Notice that menu that's appearing? That's where all the additional apps are.

MAKING CALLS

So...who you going to call? Ghostbusters?!

You would be the most awesome person in the world if Ghostbusters was in your phone contacts! But before you can find that number in your contacts, it would probably help to know how to add a contact, find a contact, edit a contact, and put contacts into groups, right? So before we get to making calls, let's do baby steps and cover Contacts.

CONTACTS

So, let's open up the Contacts app to get started. See it? Not on your favorite bar, right? So where is it?! That's why I showed you earlier how to get to additional apps. Swipe up from the middle of your Home screen and keep swiping until the menu appears in its entirety.

It's in alphabetical order, so the Contacts app is in the Cs. It looks like this:

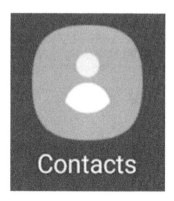

Chances are if you've added your email account, you'll already have a lot of contacts listed. Like hundreds! There's going to be a message about merging them—that's up to you.

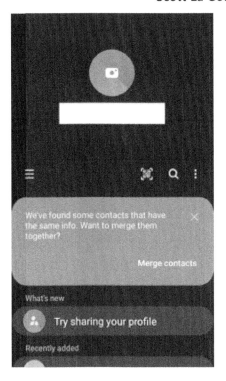

You can either search for the contact by clicking the magnifying glass, scroll slowly, or head to the right-hand side of the app and scroll—this lets you quickly scroll by letters. Just slide your finger until you see the letter of the contact you want and then stop.

I'm getting ahead of myself, however! Before you can scroll, it would be nice to know how to add a contact so there are people to scroll to. To add a contact, tap on that plus sign.

Before adding the contact, it will ask you where you want it saved—your Samsung account, the phone or Google. It's entirely up to you, but saving it to Google might save you some trouble if you switch to a different phone manufacturer in the future.

Adding a person looks more like applying for a job than adding a contact. There are rows and rows of fields!

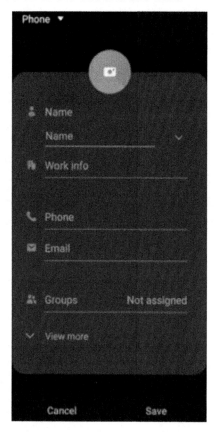

Just in case you weren't overwhelmed by all the fields, you can tap more fields and get even more!

Here's the most important thing you need to know: fields are optional! You can add a name and email and that's it. You don't even have to add their phone number. If you want to call them, then that would certainly help though.

If you have a hard time remembering who people are, then you can also take a picture or add a picture you already have. Comes in handy if you have eight kids and you can't remember if Joey is the one with blonde hair or red hair. Just tap the camera icon up top, then tap either Gallery (to assign a photo you've already taken) or Camera (to take a picture of them); you can also use one of the avatar type icons Samsung has.

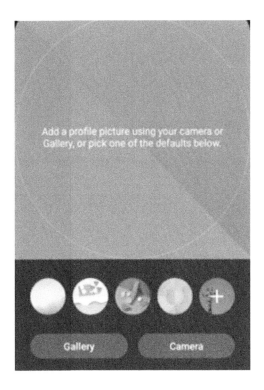

Once you are done, tap the save button.

EDITING A CONTACT

If you add an email and then later decide you should add a phone number, or if you want to edit anything else, then just find the name in your contacts and tap it once. This brings up all the info you've already added.

Go to the bottom of the screen and tap on the Edit option button. This makes the contact editable. Go to your desired field and update. When you are finished make sure to tap Save.

SHARING A CONTACT

If you have your phone long enough, someone will ask you for so-and-so's phone number. The old-fashioned way was to write it down. But you have a smartphone, so you aren't old-fashioned!

The new way to share a number is to find the person in your contacts, tap their name, then tap Share on the bottom left corner of the screen.

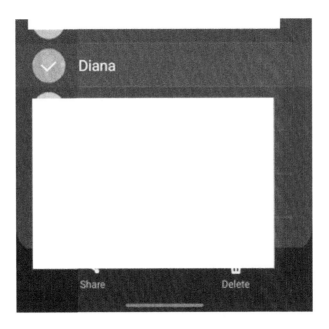

From here you have a few options, but the easiest is to text or email the contact to your friend. This sends them a contact card. So if you have other information with that contact (such as email) then that will be sent over as well.

DELETE CONTACT

Deleting a contact is the same as sharing a contact. The only difference is once you tap their name, you tap the delete icon to the right (not the share to the left). This erases them from your phone, but not your life.

GET ORGANIZED

Once you start getting lots of contacts, then it's going to make finding someone more time-consuming. Groups helps. You can add a Group for "Family" for instance, and then stick all of your family members there.

When you open your contacts and tap those three lines in the upper left corner, you'll see a menu. This is where you'll see your Groups. So with Groups, you can jump right into that list and find the contact you need.

You can also send the entire group inside the Group an email or text message. So for instance, if your child is turning two and you want to remind everyone in your "Family" contact not to come, then just tap on that Group.

But what if you don't have labels? Or if you want to add people to a label? Easy. Remember that long application you used to add a contact? One of the fields was called "Groups." You have to tap more to see it. It's all the way at the bottom. One of the last fields, in fact.

If you've never added a label or want to add a new one, then just start typing. If you have another one that you'd like to use, then just tap the arrow and select it.

When you are done, don't forget to tap Save.

You can also quickly assign someone to a group by tapping on the contact's name, then selecting Create Group from the upper right.

Once you tap that, you'll get to add a name, assign a ringtone, and assign other members.

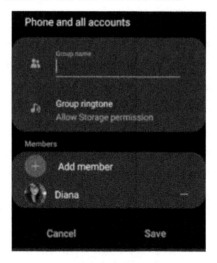

DELETE GROUP

If you decide you no longer want to have a la-bel, then just go to the menu I showed you above—side menu, then the three dots. From here, tap the Delete Group.

If there's just one person you want to boot from the label, then tap them and go to the Group and delete it.

MAKING CALLS

That concludes our sidetrack into the Contacts app. We can now get back to making phone calls to the Ghostbusters.

You can make a call by opening the Contacts app, then selecting the contact, and then tapping on their phone number. Alternatively, you can tap

on the Phone button from your Home screen or favorite bar.

There are a few options when you open this
app. Let's talk about each one.

Starting from the far left is the Keypad tab. It's
green because you are already there.

In the middle is the Recents tab. If you've made
any calls, they'll show here.

The last option is Contacts, which opens a version of the Contacts app that's within the Phone
app.

If you want to dial someone the old-fashioned
way by tapping in numbers, then tap them, and tap
the call icon. You can also tap the video icon to
start a video call.

When you are done with the call, hit the End button on your phone.

ANSWER AND DECLINE CALLS

What do you do when someone calls you? Probably ignore it because it's a telemarketer!

It's easy to accept a call, however. When the phone rings, the number will appear and if the person is in your Contacts, then the name will appear as well. To answer, just swipe the "answer." To decline just drag the "decline."

PHONE SETTINGS

If you haven't noticed already, there are settings for pretty much everything. Samsung is a *highly* customizable phone. To get to settings, go to the upper right corner, then select Settings.

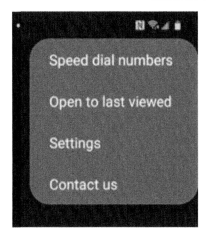

From settings you can set up ringtones, add numbers to block, set up your voicemail and much more.

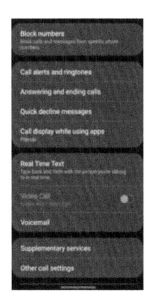

PLAY ANGRY BIRDS WHILE TALKING TO ANGRY MOM

What if you're on a call with your mom and she's just complaining about something, but you don't want to be rude and hang up? Easy. You multitask! This means you could play Angry Birds while talking!

To multitask, just swipe up from the bottom of your phone and open the app you want to work in while you are talking. The call will show in the notification area. Tap it to return to the call.

MESSAGES

Now that you know how Contacts and Phone works, messaging will be like second nature. They share many of the same properties.

Let's open up the Messages app (it's on your Favorites Bar).

CREATE / SEND A MESSAGE

When you have selected the contact(s) to send a message to, tap Compose. You can also manually type in the number in the text field.

You can add more than one contact—this is known as a group text.

The first time you send a message, it's going to probably look pretty bare like the image below. Assuming you have never sent one, it's going to be blank. Once you start getting messages, you can tap on New category to create labels for them—so all your family messages, for example, will be in one place.

Once you are ready to send your first message, tap the message icon.

The top field is where you put who it's going to (or the group name if it's several people). You can use the + icon to find people in your contacts.

Use the text field to type out your message.

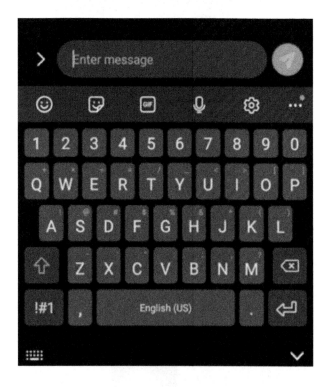

It looks pretty basic, but there's actually a *lot* here. Starting on the bottom, there's a little keyboard—that's to switch to a different type of keyboard; to the right of that is a down arrow, which will collapse the keyboard. To get it back, just click the message box again.

Just above the keyboard icon, is a !#1 button, which will switch the alpha keyboard to a numeric / symbol keyboard (so you have quick access to symbols like @, ?, %).

Typing in another language or need an accent sign? Long press the letter and you'll reveal more characters and symbols for that letter.

Finally, at the top is a set of six additional icons.

From left to right, the first is the Emoji pack. If you want to respond to someone with an Emoji, then that's what you tap.

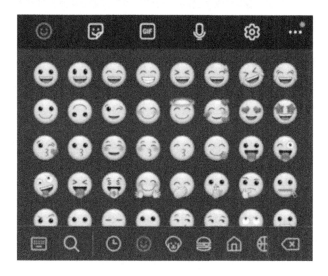

You can scroll through all of them by swiping right, but because there's so many of them, they are also grouped together, and you can jump to a group by tapping on the associated image on the bottom.

Next to the Emoji icon is the Bitmoji sticker icon. I'll cover Bitmoji later, but for now, let's just say Bitmoji is like an emoji that is customized to look like you. To use it, you have to download it. It's free.

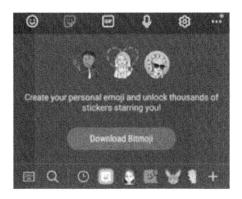

Next is the GIF search; you have to agree to the terms to use it. It's basically a search engine for GIF images; so if you want to find a birthday GIF to put in a message, for example, you could search "birthday" and see literally dozens and dozens of GIFs. If you don't know what a GIF is, they are small images that move on a loop—kind of like mini movies that last a couple seconds.

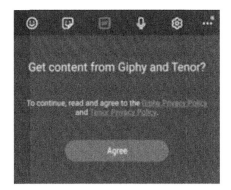

To the right of the GIF icon is the microphone icon, which lets you record a voice message instead of typing it.

You know Samsung loves its settings, so it probably won't surprise you that the config icon launches keyboard settings.

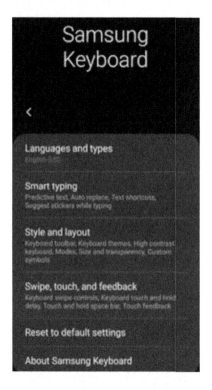

Because they love settings so much, there are a few more when you tap the three dots; you can adjust the keyboard size here, but also use some of the many other features—such as text editing and translation.

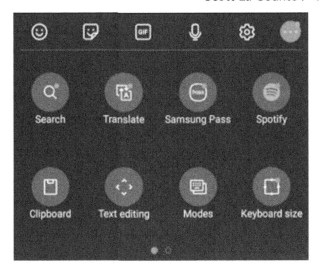

So, like I said, there's a lot to this keyboard. But the keyboard is only half the fun! Look above it…that little > icon will bring out some more things you can do with the message.

There are three additional options. The first is to include a picture that's in your photo gallery.

The next is to either take a photo or record a video.

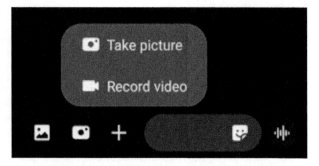

And the last is a series of extra options.

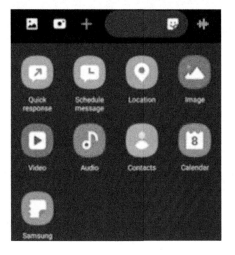

From left to right starting at the top:

- Quick response – Gives a list of common responses so you don't have to type anything.
- Schedule message – Lets you define when the message will be sent.
- Location – Shares where you are currently located with a person. So if a person is meeting you and they're saying

"I'm looking for you, but don't see you!" you can send this to give them a better idea.

- Image / Video – this is similar to adding a video / image from your gallery (you can actually do that here as well), but it also searches for them in other places like Google Drive.
- Audio – Share an audio file.
- Contacts – Share someone's contact information.
- Calendar – Share an event in your calendar with another person.
- Samsung – Share a Samsung Note with a person.

When you are ready to send your message, tap the arrow with the SMS under it.

VIEW MESSAGE

When you get a message, your phone will vibrate, chirp, or do nothing—it all depends on how you set up your phone. To view the message, you can either open the app, or swipe down to see your notifications—one will be the text message.

WHERE'S AN APP FOR THAT?

I mentioned earlier that you could play Angry Birds while talking to your angry mom on the phone. Sound fun? But where is Angry Birds on your phone? It's not! You have to download it.

Adding and removing apps on the Galaxy is easy. Head to your favorite bar on the bottom of your Home screen and tap the Google Play app.

This launches the Play Store.

From here you can browse the top apps, see editors' picks, look through categories, or, if you have an app in mind, search for it. The Play Store isn't just for apps. You can use the tabs on the top to go to movies, books, and music. Any kind of downloadable content that's offered by Google can be found here.

When you see the app you want, tap on it. You can read through reviews, see screenshots, and install it on your phone. To install, simply tap the install button—if it's a paid app you'll be prompted to buy it. If there's no price, it's free (or offers in-app payments—which means the app is free, but there are premium features inside it you may have to pay for).

The app is now stored in the app section of your device (remember the section you get to when you swipe up from the bottom to the top?).

REMOVE APP

If you decide you no longer want an app, go to the app in the app menu and tap and hold it. This brings up a box with a few options. The one you want is Uninstall.

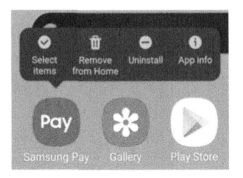

If you downloaded the app from the Play Store, you can always delete it. Some apps that were pre-installed on your phone cannot be deleted.

DRIVING DIRECTIONS

Back in the day, you may have had a GPS. It was a fancy plastic device that would give you directions for anywhere in North America. You can throw out that device because your phone is your new GPS.

To get directions, swipe up to open up your apps, and go to the Google folder. Tap the Maps app.

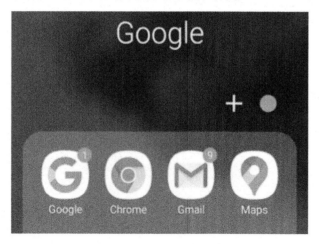

It's automatically going to be set to wherever you are currently at—which is both creepy and useful.

To get started, just type where you want to go. I'm searching for Disneyland, Anaheim.

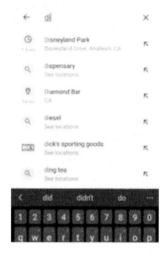

It automatically starts filling in what it thinks you are going to type and tells you the distance. When you see the one you want, tap it.

It pinpoints the location on the map and also gives you an option to call, share or get directions to the location. If you want to zoom out or in, just use two fingers and pinch in or out on the screen.

It automatically gets directions from where you are. Want it from a different location? Just tap on the "Your location" field and type where you want to go. You can also reverse the directions by tapping on the double arrows. When you are ready to go, tap Start.

What if you don't want to drive? What if you want to walk? Or bike? Or take a taxi? There are options for all of those and more! Tap the slider un-der the address bar to whatever you prefer. This updates the directions—when you walk, for example, it will show you one-way streets and also update the time it will take you.

What if you want to drive but are like me: terrified of freeways in California? There's an option to avoid highways. Tap the menu button in the upper right corner of the screen and select Route options (there are actually lots of other things packed in here like adding stops, sharing directions, and sharing your location).

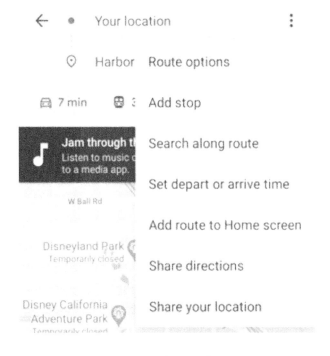

In the Route options, select what you want to avoid, and hit Done. You are now rerouted to a longer route—notice how the times probably changed?

Once you get your directions, you can swipe up to get turn-by-turn directions.

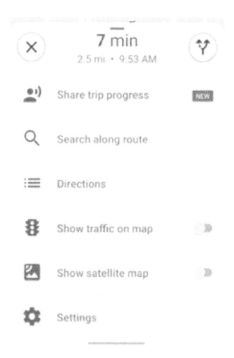

You can even see what it looks like from the street. It's called Street View.

Street View isn't only for streets. Google is expanding the feature everywhere. If you hold your finger over the map, there will be an option to show Street View if it's available. Just tap the thumbnail. Here's a Street View of Disneyland:

You can wander around the entire park! If only you could ride the rides, too! You can get even closer to the action by picking up the Dreamview headset. When you stick your phone in that, you can turn your head and the view turns with you.

Street View is also available in a lot of malls and other tourist attractions. Point your map to the Smithsonian in Washington, DC and get a pretty cool Street View.

LIVE CAPTIONING

One of the bigger features to Android 10 is live captioning; live captioning can transcribe any video you record and show what's being said. It works surprisingly well and is pretty accurate.

To turn it on, go to Settings > Accessibility > Hearing enhancements > Live caption.

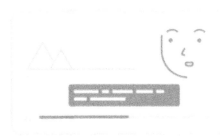

In the settings, you can also toggle off profanity, and, coming soon, select a different language. If it's something you'd only occasionally use, I recommend leaving it toggled off, but having it toggled on under Live Caption in volume control. With that toggled on, all you have to do is press the volume button. Once you do that, you'll see the option to turn it on; it's the bottom option.

Once it's on, you'll start seeing a transcription appear in seconds.

REFRESH RATE

The Galaxy supports up to 120Hz refresh rate. Wow, right? Actually, most people have no idea what this means. It's frames per second (FPS)—or 120 FPS. So, what does that mean? If you're playing games or using something that has fast moving action, it means things will seem a lot smoother. It will also eat your battery life to shreds, so use with caution (60Hz is the norm). The battery life for 120 FPS is much better on newer Galaxy phones.

To toggle it on go to Settings > Display > Motion smoothness.

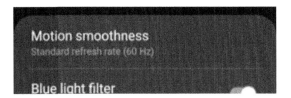

Next, select 120 Hz.

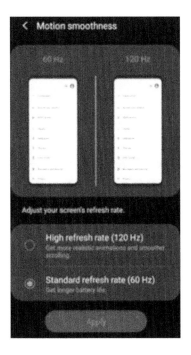

I recommend turning it on just to see what it looks like, but if you are not just absolutely blown away by it, then turn it off so you can have a longer lasting battery.

SHARING WI-FI

Anytime you have guests over, you almost always get the question: what's your wi-fi password? If you are like me, then it probably annoys you. Maybe your password is really long, maybe you just don't like giving out your password, or maybe you are just too embarrassed to say that it's "Feet$Fet-ishLover1." Whatever the reason, then you will love sharing your wi-fi with QR codes. Gone are the days of giving this info out. Just give them a code that they scan, and they'll have access without ever knowing what your password is.

To use it, go to your wi-fi settings, then select the Wi-Fi options and Wi-Fi Direct.

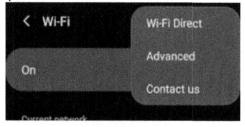

Make sure both devices have Wi-Fi on and follow the directions.

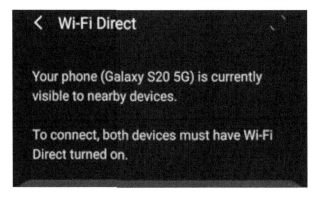

KIDS HOME

One place Samsung truly shines above other companies is with its parental control features and kids mode. Yes, other devices have parental controls, but Samsung takes it up a notch by creating a UI that's just for kids.

With kids mode, you can quickly toggle it on and off for those moments where you need to distract a child.

To access it, swipe down to bring down your notification bar, then swipe right one time. It's one of the notifications icons that you'll need to manually add to use.

The first time you launch it, you'll have to download a very small program. It will take a few seconds depending on your connection speed.

Once it's done downloading, you'll see the welcome screen and be asked if you want to create a shortcut on your desktop. Tap Start when you are ready.

Once you tap Next, you'll get to the main Samsung Kids UI. It looks a little like your phone...only cuter! There's a handful of icons on the screen, but you'll notice they each have download buttons. That's because they aren't installed yet. You have to tap the download button for each app you want to install (not more than three at a time).

Swipe to your left, and you'll see non-Samsung apps. These need to be downloaded as well.

You might be thinking, how safe can this mode be? There's an Internet browser right on the Home screen! Tap it and let's see!

You'll notice right away that this is not yo mama's Internet! The only websites they can access are the ones you add. Want to add one? Tap the +New website button.

You'll quickly notice that all the apps in this mode are very stripped down. Even the camera app, which is pretty harmless, has few features. There's a shutter, a toggle for photos and videos, and a button for effects.

The phone is the same way. Your child can't open the app and call anyone. They can only call numbers that you've added. Want to add someone? Just tap the + icon.

The pre-installed apps are all pretty harmless, and borderline educational.

If there's apps you want to remove or install, then tap the option button in the upper right corner.

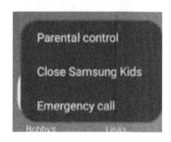

Once you put in your pin, you'll have access to the settings. Here you'll be able to control what your child does and how long they do it for. You can also monitor what they've been doing. You can control how much time they can spend on something like games and something like reading.

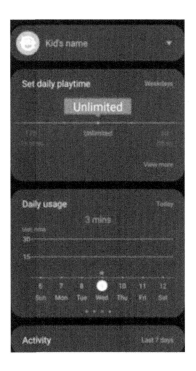

Is there a pre-installed app that you don't want your child to see? No problem! Scroll down a little and tap the Apps option.

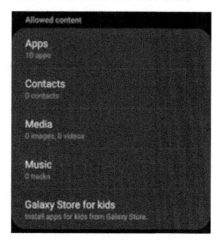

From the options button, select Remove and then select the app that you want removed.

What about other apps? Like third-party ones? Return to that list and select Galaxy Store for kids. That's going to take you to a custom kids' store. It's not going to have teen or adult games—it's only games that are appropriate for kids.

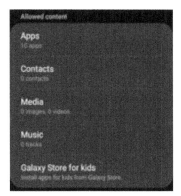

Tap the download option next to any app that you want to download. They'll show up when you swipe right from kids Home screen.

So that's all well and good, but what happens when you want to return to adulthood? How do you get out of this mode? It takes just a second! On the Home screen, tap the back icon. It will ask you for your pin code. Once you add it, you are back in normal mode. That's it!

SMARTTAGS

If you bought your Galaxy phone when it was first released, then chances are it was bundled with a SmartTag; if not, it is $29.99.

SmartTag is an optional accessory for finding your gadgets and devices. You can attach it to your king ring, stick it on a remote, put it in your purse, or wherever you might lose something. If you can't find your keys, then from your phone you can ping it and the SmartTag will start ringing.

You can also connect your SmartTag to smart home devices like lights and doors; so when you come up, you can double click your tag to perform an action—like turn on the lights.

SmartTag connects to your phone with Bluetooth and runs on a battery. As long as you aren't pinging your device every five minutes, you shouldn't have to replace the battery very often.

To get started, go to the SmartThings app from the Samsung folder of all apps; if you don't have it, you can download it free from the app store. It's included with the newest OS update, so chances are it's there if you have a new phone.

The first time the app opens, you'll have to agree to the terms and conditions.

Once you click start, press the button on the tag and it should find it right away. Make sure and tap "While using the app" on the next screen.

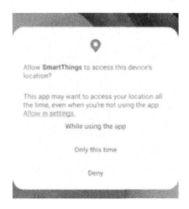

If the tag will always be in a particular room, then you can name it; otherwise just skip it.

Next it will ask if you want to add the device now or later. Tap Add Now.

Next, confirm that the tag can know your location. It needs to know the location to propertly work.

Click start next.

It will take a few seconds to set everything up.

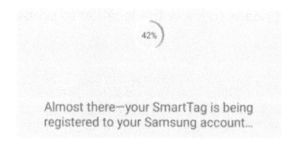

When it's done, you'll be prompted to name the tag. You can keep it as SmartTag, but being more descriptive (i.e. calling it car keys) is advisable if you have several SmartTag's.

You'll see a couple of setup screens, then it will ask you if you want to update the SmartTag; I recommend doing this. It is very quick and it makes sure the SmartTag is free of any bugs.

Once it's done, you'll see your main screen; click Get Started.

Next, download the add-on software.

Once you're finished, you can open the software again and you'll be able to tap the music icon to ping your SmartTag; when you do, it will start to ring.

[5]

INTERNET

This chapter will cover:
- Setting up email
- Creating and sending email
- Managing multiple accounts
- Browsing the Internet

When it comes to the Internet, there are two things you'll want to do:
- Send email
- Browse the Internet

ADD AN EMAIL ACCOUNT

When you set up your phone, you'll set it up to your Google Account, which is usually your email.

You may, however, want to add another email account—or remove the one you set up.

To add an email, swipe up to bring up your apps, and tap on Settings.

Next, tap on Accounts.

From here, select Add Account; you can also tap on the account that's been set up and tap re-move account—but remember you can have more than one account on your phone.

Once you add your email, you'll be asked what type of email it is. Follow the steps after you select the email type to add in your email, password, and other required fields.

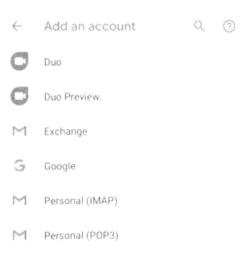

CREATE AND SEND AN EMAIL

To send an email using Gmail (Samsung's native email app), swipe up to get to your apps, tap Gmail, and tap Compose a New Email (the little round, red pencil in the lower right corner). When you're done, tap the Send button.

You can also use the Google Play Store to find other email apps (such as Outlook).

MANAGE MULTIPLE EMAIL ACCOUNTS

If you have more than one Gmail account, tap the three lines at the upper left of your email screen; this brings out a slider menu. If you tap on the little arrow next to the email address, it drops down and will show other accounts. If none are listed, you can add one.

SURFING THE INTERNET

Google's native Web browser is Chrome. You can use other browsers (which can be found in the Google Play Store). This book will only cover Chrome, however.

Get started by tapping on the Chrome browser icon from your favorite bar, or by going into all programs.

If you've used Chrome on a desktop or any other device, then this chapter won't exactly be rocket science—just like the email app, many of the same properties you find on the desktop exist on the mobile version.

When you open it, you'll see it's a pretty basic browser. There are three main things that you'll want to note.

- **Address Bar** - As you would guess, this is where you put the Internet address you want to go to (google.com, for example); what you should understand, however is that this is not just an address bar. This is a search bar. You can use it to search for things just as you would searching for something on Google; when you hit the enter key, it takes you to the Google search results page.

- **Tab Button** - Because you are limited in space, you don't actually see all your tabs like you would on a normal browser; instead you get a button that tells you how many tabs are open. If you tap it, you can either toggle between the tabs, or swipe over one of the pages to close the tab.

- **Menu Button** - The last button brings up a menu with a series of other options that I'll talk about next.

☆   ↓   ⓘ   ↻

New tab

New incognito tab

Bookmarks

Recent tabs

History

Downloads

Share

Find in page

Add to Home screen

Desktop site   ☐

Settings

Help & feedback

The menu is pretty straightforward, but there are a few things worth noting.

"New incognito tab" opens your phone into private browsing; that doesn't mean your IP isn't tracked. It means your history isn't record; it also means passwords and cookies aren't stored.

A little bit further down is "History"; if you want your history erased so there's no record on your phone of where you went, then go here and clear your browsing history.

History   ⓘ   Q   ✕

Your Google Account may have other forms of browsing history at myactivity.google.com

CLEAR BROWSING DATA

If you want to erase more than just websites (passwords, for example) then go to Settings at the very bottom of the menu. This opens up more advanced settings.

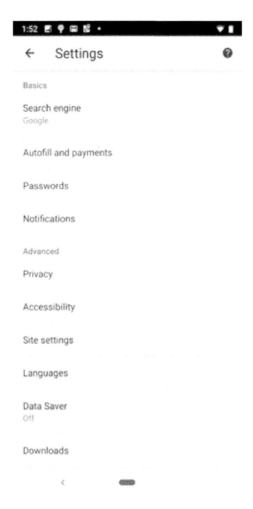

[6]
SNAP IT!

This chapter will cover:
- How to take different photos
- How to take videos
- Camera settings
- Different camera features

The camera is the bread and butter of the Samsung phone. Many people consider the Samsung Galaxy to be the greatest camera ever on a phone. I'll leave that for you to decide. Personally, I think all top tier phone cameras have their own pros and cons.

This chapter is based off the Galaxy Ultra. As mentioned earlier in the book, not all smartphones are alike in terms of cameras; it's one of the most noticeable differences with the phones. The Ultra has more lens, more zoom and more pixels.

This means that if you are using a non-Ultra phone, some of the things mentioned in this chapter won't apply to you. So if you are reading and thinking "where is that on my phone" then you probably don't have an Ultra.

THE BASICS

Are you ready to get your Ansel Adams on? Let's get started by opening the Camera app

When you open the app, it starts in the basic camera mode. The UI can look pretty simple, but don't be fooled. There are a lot of controls.

On the bottom of the screen is the shutter (to take your photo)—swipe it down to take a "burst shot" which takes several photos at once, and hold it down to toggle to video. To the right of the shutter is the camera flip—to switch to the front camera.

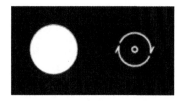

Up on the top of the camera app is where you'll find the majority of your settings.

Starting from left to right, there is the settings icon. Most of the settings are just toggle switches and easy to understand.

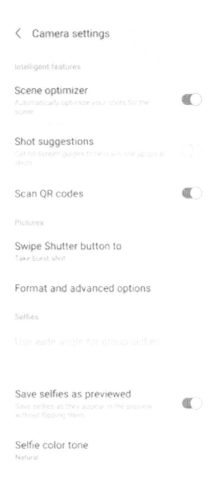

Next to that is the flash setting. Tapping that will let you select no flash, auto flash, or force flash.

The next option is the timer. This lets you delay when the photo will be taken. It's best used with a tripod.

The next option lets you pick how large the photo will be. The best option is 108 MB. That's going to give you an unbelievably *huge* image. It's also going to take away the next two options. If you notice they're grayed out...that's why. This is the only mode that you cannot use them on.

And what are those two options? The first toggles Motion on and off. And the second lets you use special filters to enhance the photo.

One final note on photos (and this applies to videos as well): to zoom, you pinch in and out.

CAMERA MODES

Taking pictures is so yesterday though, isn't it? Smartphones are loaded with different modes and Samsung is obviously no stranger to some really great ones.

Think of modes like different lenses. You have your basic camera lens, but then you can also have a lens for fisheye and close up. If you look at the bottom of your camera app, you can slide left and right to get to the different modes.

There are three main ones in the app: photos (which I covered above), videos, and Single Take.

If you've had a smartphone before, then video will probably be familiar to you, but Single Take will probably be new.

Quickly, the video mode has similar features to photo mode. Starting at the bottom, you can pick the kind of video you are taking—three leaves will pull the zoom back and give a wider shot, and one leaf will pull it in and give a closer one.

Up on top, the menu is largely the same as the photo one.

I'll point out one thing, however: the 9:16 icon will launch the video ratio. Video can actually record all the way to 8K! But be careful! As you probably can guess, an 8K video is going to be *huge*. One advantage to that mode is you are able to pull pretty good still photos from the video.

Just like the other modes, pinching in and out will let you zoom in and out.

Single Take is a pretty cool mode. When you press it, it starts recording a 15 second clip. There are no filters or ratios you can change here. It's stripped down.

The beauty of this mode is what it's doing is using a computer to pick the best photo from the video. When the fifteen seconds are up, it will start populating them.

If you click the More option on the slider, you'll see that there are actually several more photography modes on the phone. Twelve more modes to be exact.

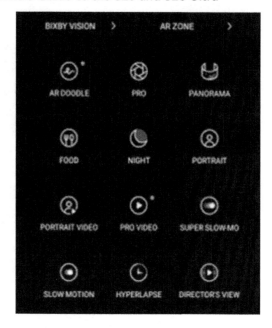

AR Doodle used to be a feature in video recording, but it's now been moved to its own camera mode. The mode let's draw things as you record.

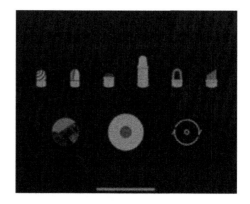

If you thought the Photo mode was a little lacking in options and settings, wait until you see the Pro mode!

You can adjust things like ISO, auto focus and more.

There's also a Pro Video mode with a similar feature set.

Panorama lets you create a panoramic photo; it's great for landscape and cityscape shots.

Food changes settings to give the most ideal focus and effects to take food photos.

Night mode will help you get great shots in low lighting.

Portrait and Portrait Video (previously called Live Focus and Live Focus Video) are great for close up shots of people where you want to blur the background.

Super Slow-Mo, Slow motion and Hyperlapse let you capture either slow motion videos or time-lapse videos.

The final mode is called Director's View, and it's pretty awesome! It lets you record video with both the front and back facing camera at the same time. It's perfect for capturing people's reaction, doing tours, and more. When you use it, you'll see the main screen, then the other camera in the lower left corner.

Tap the arrow above Director's View to toggle between the camera you are using. Just tap the preview to switch.

EXPERT RAW

You might be familiar with RAW; but Expert RAW? What's that all about? Shooting in RAW is something only on the Ultra Samsung devices; it's a professional camera setting that uses much more data than a traditional JPEG photo–to be clear: this is something you want to be careful with because it's going to take up much more space and be harder to share.

By default the camera will shoot with a traditional JPEG or HEIC file format. When it does this, it's creating a single file format. It's perfect for most people. But photographers like to edit photos, and that's where Expert RAW comes in. Expert RAW creates a multi-frame, which gives much more flexibility for editing a photo.

Expert Raw used to be an app you downloaded from the app store; but with One UI 5.1, it is now integrated into the camera app–while still an app in itself. To use it (if your phone supports it), go to the More tab in the camera app; the setting is a shortcut and will take you to the Expert Raw app–a download may be needed.

COLOR TONE ON SELFIE

The Selfie camera features two color tones: Natural and Bright. By default, Natural Tone is selected. As the name implies, bright will brighten up your normal tone.

To use it turn on the selfie camera, then tap the effects button in the top right corner (looks a little like a wand). From here, select the Color Tone option, then toggle between Natural or Bright.

EDITING PHOTOS

Once you take a photo, you can begin fine-tuning it to really make it sparkle. You can access editing by opening the photo you want to make edits to. This is done by either opening it from the camera app by clicking on the photo preview (next to the shutter):

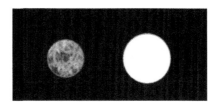

Or by opening the Photo app.

Later in this chapter, I'll write a bit more about how photos are organized, and how you can change things around. For now, we are just talking about editing a photo, so for the purpose of this section, tap on any photo to edit it.

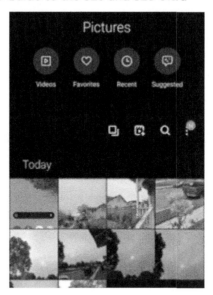

When you open a photo, the options you see will vary depending on what kind of photo you open.

The below example is a Live Focus photo.

As the name suggests, the background is blurred. There's also an option here: Change background effect. This technically isn't editing a photo—when you edit a photo, you go into a different app.

When you tap change the background, you'll have four options. With each option, you can change the intensity of the blur with the slider.

The main blur is simply called "blur"; the next is a spin blur.

The third is a zoom blur.

The last type of blur is color point, which makes the object color and the background black and white.

If you make any changes here, always make sure and tap Apply to save it.

Single Take photos also work a little differently when it comes to editing because you have to select which photo you want to edit.

Regardless of the type of photo, there are going to be several options that are the same. Starting on the top, that little play icon will wirelessly show your photo on another device (like a compatible TV).

Next to the play icon is an icon that looks kind of like an eye. That will digitally scan your photo and try and identify what the photo is. In the below example, it finds a flower and gives a link to see more. This feature works pretty well, but isn't always perfect.

Next to the eye icon is an option icon. This will let you set a photo as wallpaper, print it, etc. If you tap Details, it will also let you see when the photo was taken, its resolution, and any tags that have been assigned to it.

On the bottom of any photo are four additional options. The heart icon favorites the photo, the pencil lets you edit it (more on that in a second), the three dots lets you share it, and the trash lets you delete it.

Tap the pencil icon and let's see how to edit a photo next. Regardless of the photo, you'll see the same options on the bottom.

The first option is to crop the photo. To crop, drag the little white corners.

Next is the filter option. The slider lets you select the type of filter, and below that is a slider to adjust the intensity of the filter.

Brightness is the next icon. Each icon here adjusts a different setting (such as the contrast of the photo).

The sticker icon will launch Bitmoji (I'll discuss this later in the chapter), but what this does is let you put stickers on top of your photo.

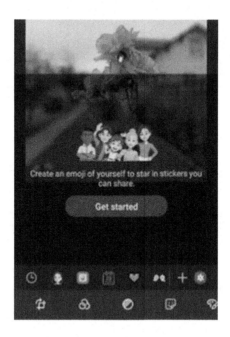

The paintbrush icon lets you draw on top of your photo.

And the text icon lets you write on top of your photo.

If you don't want to spend time editing your photo—you just want it to magically look better with no effort, there's an option up in the upper left corner that will do that for you—it crops, rotates, and adds a filter to it. Depending on how well you took the shot, you may not see much difference.

In the upper right corner is an options menu with even more choices for editing your picture.

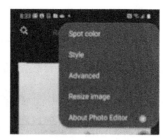

The first is Spot color. Using the little pickers, you can remove a color from the photo to make the subject stand out. To save any changes here, make sure and tap the checkmark; to cancel changes, tap the X.

Style applies filters that give the photo more of an artistic pop—if you want your photo to look like a painting, for example. The slider below it will adjust the intensity.

The advanced option will let you do color corrections.

If you took a photo at the highest resolution and are having difficulty sharing it, you can use the Resize image option to make it smaller.

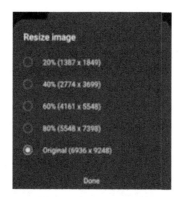

Once you are finished doing edits, make sure and tap Save.

EDITING VIDEOS

Editing a video shares a lot of common features to photos, so make sure and read that section first, as I will not repeat features already referenced above.

To get started open the video that you want to edit, then tap to play it. In the play window, there are going to be a couple of things you should note.

Over on the upper left side you'll see the icon below. This lets you capture a photo from the video. You can do it with any resolution, but you'll find the best photos will come from an 8K video.

Over on the upper right side is a GIF button. This will let you create a GIF from your video.

You'll notice the video has the same options at the bottom of it (assuming you haven't played it). To edit it, just tap on that pencil.

The first option you'll see is to crop the video. To crop just drag in or out the white bars before and after the video clip.

Next is the color filter, which works almost identically to the photo filter.

The text icon comes after this and lets you write on top of the photo.

The emoji sticker insert is after this.

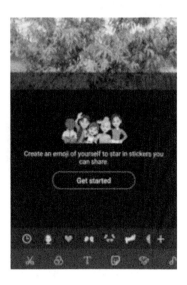

And the paintbrush is second to last.

The last icon is for adding sound. You can add music or anything else you want. You can also use the slider under Video sound to make the videos original sound softer (or nonexistent)—so, for example, you could remove all sound from a family dinner, and replace it with music.

Up on top, there's one option: resolution. If you've recorded in 8K and it's too large, you can use this option to make it smaller.

CUT OUT SUBJECT FROM PHOTO

If you long-press over the subject of a photo and wait, the object will be cutout of the photo and you can paste it anywhere else–such as a Google Doc or email; when it's pasted, only the subject will appear–the background will be removed.

ORGANIZING YOUR PHOTOS AND VIDEOS

The great thing about mobile photos is you always have a camera ready to capture memorable events; the bad thing about mobile photos is you always have a camera ready to capture events, and you'll find you have hundreds and hundreds of photos very quickly.

Fortunately, Samsung makes it very simple to organize your photos so you can find what you are looking for.

Let's open up the Gallery app and see how to get things organized.

Galaxy keeps things pretty simple by having only four options on the bottom of your screen.

There are four additional options up on top.

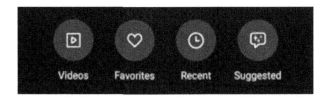

In the upper right corner, there's three dots, which is the photo option menu; that menu is there no matter where you are in the Gallery app.

When you tap that menu, you'll get several more options. From this menu you can share an album, create a GIF / collage / Slideshow of the album, or edit the photos / videos in it.

If there's something you are trying to find, tap on the magnifying glass. You can search by what it is (a Live Focus, video, etc.), you can search for tags, you can type an expression (happy photos, for example).

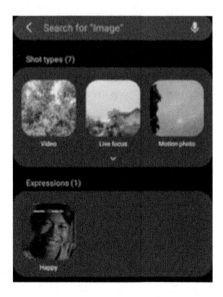

When you tap on Albums, you'll see your albums (Samsung will automatically create some for you), and you can tap on options to create a new album.

Stories lets you capture all your life adventures; you can create a new Story the same way you created an album.

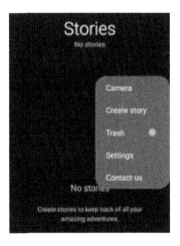

The last option is sharing your photos. To get started, tap the red button

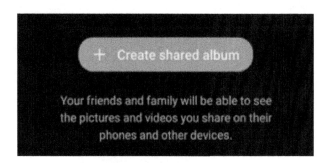

Next, type in a person's phone number or Samsung ID.

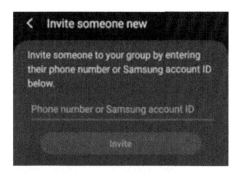

Once you have your shared album created, you can tap the + icon to add photos to it.

You don't have to add all the photos at once. You can continue to add them over time.

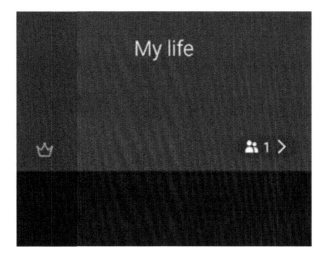

GALLERY SEARCH

Searching for photos is different than what you might be used to–or rather smarter than what you are used to. You can search for specific locations and people, but you can also search for items–so if the person was wearing sunglasses or a jacket.

BITMOJI

Bitmoji is the Samsung equivalent of Memoji on the iPhone; it basically lets you create an avatar of yourself that you can use in photos and text messages.

To get started, go to the Camera app, then select More, and finally tap AR Zone.

Next, tap the AR Emoji Camera option.

Before you can have fun, you'll need to take a picture of yourself. Make sure you are in an area with good lighting for the best results.

Position your face in the center of the screen

Once you take the photo, select the gender icon. They are as follows: adult male, adult female, male child, female child. Once you make your selecttion, you'll need wait a few seconds for it to analyze the photo.

Next, you can start using the options to change the way you look and what your avatar is wearing.

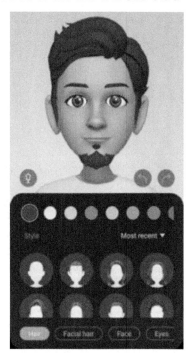

You will now be able to use your AR Camera to take photos with your avatar's head replacing other people's heads!

You can also slide over and select other pre-made avatars. My favorite is the Disney one.

On the bottom of the camera is a slider to select the different AR Camera modes. Mirror, for example, will put your avatar in the frame of the photo.

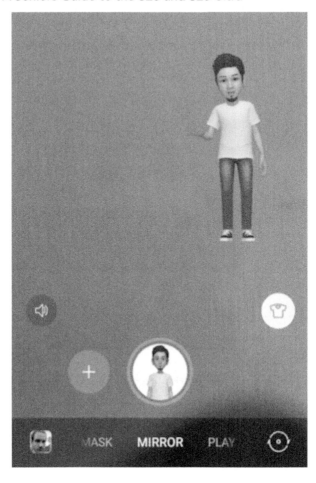

[7]
GOING BEYOND

This chapter will cover:
- System settings

If you want to take total control of your Samsung, then you need to know where the system settings are and what can and can't be changed there.

First, the easy part: the system settings are located with the rest of your apps. Swipe up and scroll down to "Settings."

This opens all the settings available:

- Connections
- Sounds and vibrations
- Notifications
- Display
- Wallpaper
- Themes
- Home screen
- Lock screen
- Biometrics and security
- Privacy
- Location
- Accounts and backup
- Google
- Advanced features
- Digital Wellbeing and parental controls
- General Management
- Apps
- Battery and Device Management
- Accessibility
- Software update
- Tips and help
- About phone

I'll cover what each setting does in this chapter. There's a lot of settings! Need to find something quickly? Use the magnifying glass up top. Before looking at the settings, however, tap the avatar of the person in the upper right corner. That's going to let you add in personal information.

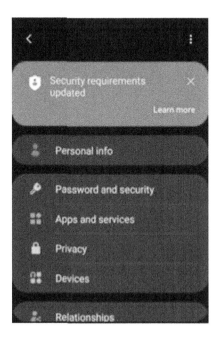

CONNECTIONS

This setting, like most settings, does exactly what it sounds like: it manages how things connect to the Internet, Bluetooth, and NFC payments (i.e. mobile credit cards).

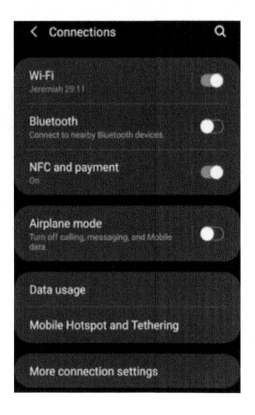

Data usage tells you how much data you've used; tapping on it gives you a deeper overview, so you can see exactly which apps used the data. Why is this important? For most, it probably won't be. I'll give an example of when it helped me: I work on the go a lot; I use the wireless on my phone to con-nect my laptop (which is called tethering); my Mac-Book was set to back up to the cloud, and little did I know it was doing this while connecting to my phone...20GB later, I was able to pinpoint what happened by looking at the data.

Below this is Hotspot and tethering. This is when you use your phone's data to connect other devices; you can use your phone's data plan, for example, to use the Internet on your iPad. Some carriers charge extra for this—mine (AT&T) includes it in the plan. To use it, tap the setting and turn it on, then name your network and password. From your other device, you find the network you set up, and connect.

Airplane mode is next. This setting turns off all wireless activity with a switch. So if you're flying and they tell you to turn everything wireless off, you can do it with a switch.

Finally, More connection settings is for doing some wireless connecting on a private network. This is not something a beginning user would need to do, and I'm not going to cover it, as the point of this book is to keep it ridiculously simple. You can also set up wireless printing and wireless emergency alerts here.

SOUNDS AND VIBRATIONS

There's a volume button on the side of your phone, so why would you need to open up a setting for it?! This setting lets you get more specific about your volume.

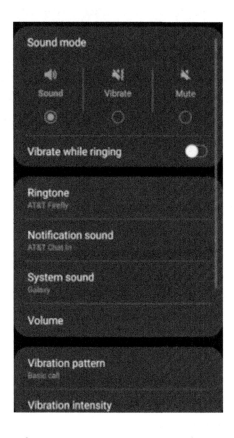

For example, you may want your alarm to ring super loud in the morning, but you want your music to play very low.

You can also use these settings to adjust the intensity of vibrations.

NOTIFICATIONS

Notifications are those pop-ups that give you alerts—like new text messages or emails. In the notification setting you can turn them off for some apps while leaving them on for others. You can also enable Do not disturb mode, which will silence all notifications.

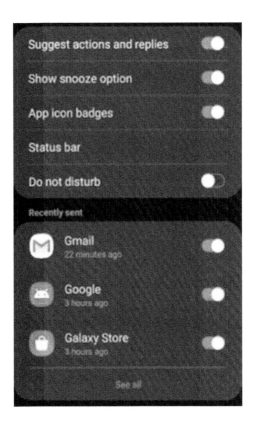

DISPLAY

As with many of the settings, almost all the main features of the Display setting can be changed outside of the app (in the notifications drop-down, for example).

This is where you'll be able to toggle on dark mode, adjust the brightness, turn on adaptive brightness, adjust the refresh rate, and toggle blue light on and off.

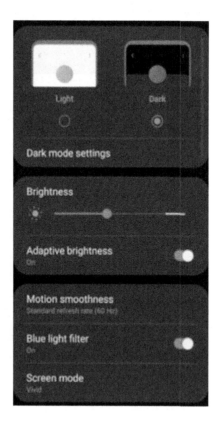

WALLPAPER / THEMES

I'm bundling these two settings together because we've talked about each of them in the section on changing your theme and wallpaper. There are no extra settings here.

HOME SCREEN

This is where you adjust your grid layout (how icons are organized and hide various apps.

LOCK SCREEN

When your phone is on standby and you lift it up: that's your lock screen. It's the screen you see before you unlock it and get to your Home screen.

The settings here change what shows up there; you can also adjust your lock setting—if, for example, you have a Face ID and want to change it to a pin ID.

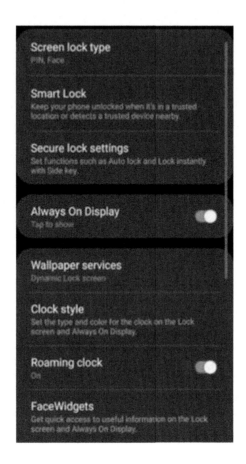

WALKING MONITOR

Do you walk and text? Your phone can tell you! Go into Digital Wellbeing, then tap on Walking monitor; not only does it track your walking time, but it tracks how often you are using your phone while walking. Watch out for that wall!

ROUTINES

Routines are what used to be known as Bixby Routines. It lets you add different modes for what you do. You can, for example, have a Work mode which has a set wallpaper and different settings; or a Sleep mode that turns off notifications.

You can access them in Settings > Modes and Routines.

Modes and Routines

⟨   Q   ⋮

Choose a mode based on what you're doing or where you are. Your phone's settings will change to match your activity or situation.

🛏   Sleep

Routines is on the bottom; when you tap the tab, you'll be able to add a new routine. Routines let you add triggers for when you do things. For example, you can set a routine for When your battery level is at 5%, turn on Power saving mode.

BIXBY TEXT CALL

AI has made big enhancements, and this is clear with Bixby Text Call. This settings let's your phone answer calls for you; it's great for blocking out SPAM. To try it, you'll want to head into your call settings, then Bixby Text Call; from here you can toggle it on and off and adjust the settings.

BIOMETRICS AND SECURITY

If you want to add a fingerprint or an additional person to Face ID, you can do so in this menu. You can also update your own—if you didn't do it with glasses, for example, then go here to redo it. You can also toggle on Find My Mobile, which lets you trace where your phone is if you've misplaced it or left it behind.

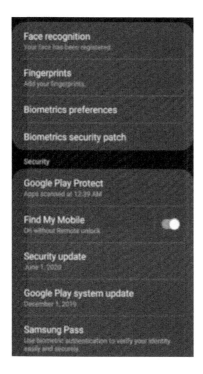

PRIVACY

Like Location Control (covered below), Privacy settings got a big upgrade in Android 10. It's so big, it now fills an entire section in the settings.

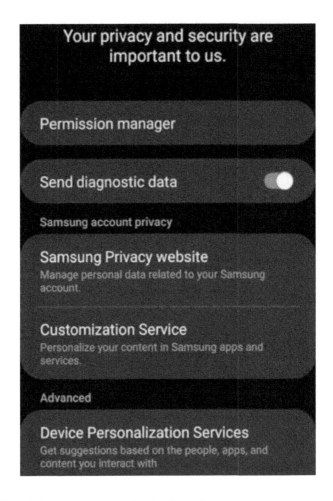

The biggest upgrade is the ability to customize what apps see what; it's no longer all or nothing. You can refine exactly how much or how little each app can see.

Tap on Permissions as one example of what you can control.

LOCATION

In the past, Location Control was an all or nothing feature—you'd decide if an app could see you all the time or none of the time. That's nice for privacy, but not nice for when you actually need someone to know your location—like when you are getting picked up by a ride app like Lyft. The new Android OS adds a new option for while you are using the app. So, for example, a ride app can only see your location while you are using the app; once the ride is over, they can no longer see what you are doing.

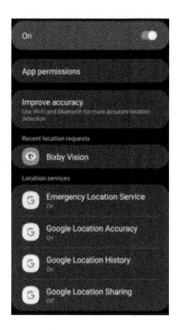

ACCOUNTS & BACKUP

If you have more than one Google account, you can tap on this to add it. If you want to remove your current account, tap on it and tap Remove—remember, however, you can have more than one account. Don't remove it just so you can add another.

You can also come here to back up your phone. It's good to do it once a month or so, but you definitely want to do it before switching to a new device.

GOOGLE

Google is where you will go to manage any Google device connected with your phone. If you are using a Google watch, for example, or a Chromecast.

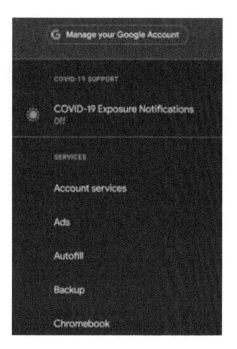

ADVANCED FEATURES

Most the features in Advanced Features are exactly what they sound: Advanced. They're features that novice users will likely never use. Things like screenshot recording features and reducing animations.

There's one important one here. One I recommend everyone use: Side key.

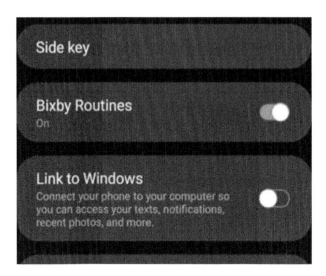

Side key is that button below the volume. Right now, if you hold it down, it goes to Bixby. Bixby isn't Samsung's most popular feature. Some people like it—many don't. If you want to change that button to power down your phone instead, then click that.

When you double tap the button, it launches the camera. You can update that too.

DIGITAL WELLBEING AND PARENTAL CONTROLS

Digital Wellbeing is my least favorite feature on the Samsung phone; now when my wife says, "You spend too much time on your phone"—she can actually prove it! The purpose of the setting is to help you manage your time more. It lets you know you're spending 12 hours a day updating your social media with memes of cats, and "hopefully" make you feel like perhaps you shouldn't do that.

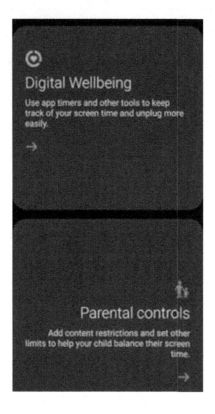

If you have kids using your phone, this is where you can also set up parental controls.

BATTERY AND DEVICE CARE

Samsung tries to make it simple to take care of your phone. With one click (the blue Optimize now), you can have your phone scanned and any problematic apps will be closed.

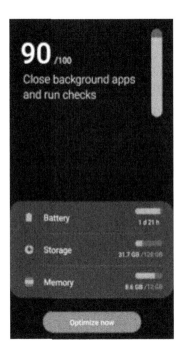

You can also tap on any of the three sections: Battery, Storage, and Memory.

The battery setting is more about analytics than settings you can change. There are some settings here you can edit—you can put your phone in battery saving mode, for example. This setting is more useful if your battery is draining too quickly; it helps you troubleshoot what's going on so you can get more life from your phone.

When you first get your phone, storage won't be a big issue, but once you start taking photos (which are larger than you think) and installing apps, it's going to go very quickly.

The storage setting helps you manage this. It shows you what's taking up storage, so you can decide if you want to delete things. Just tap on any of the subsections and follow the instructions for what to do to save space.

APPS

Every app you download has different settings and permissions. A map app, for example, needs your permission to know your location. You can turn these permissions on and off here. Does it really matter? App makers can't abuse it, right? Sort of. Here's an example: a few months ago, a popular ride-sharing app made headlines because it wanted to know where passengers were after they left the ride, so they could promote different restaurants and stores and make even more money. Many felt this was both greedy and an invasion of privacy; if you are of the latter stance, then you could go in here and stop sharing your location.

How? Just tap Advanced then look at all the permissions you are giving away. Go to the permission you are concerned with and toggle the app from on to off.

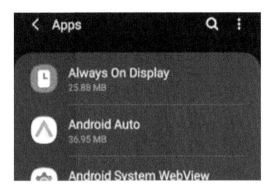

GENERAL MANAGEMENT

General management is where you go to change the language and date / time; the most important thing here, however, is Reset. This is where you can do a complete factory reset of your phone.

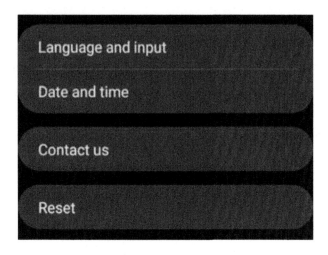

ACCESSIBILITY

Do you hate phones because the text is too small, the colors are all wrong, you can't hear anything? Or something else? That's where accessibility can help. This is where you make changes to the device to make it easier on your eyes or ears.

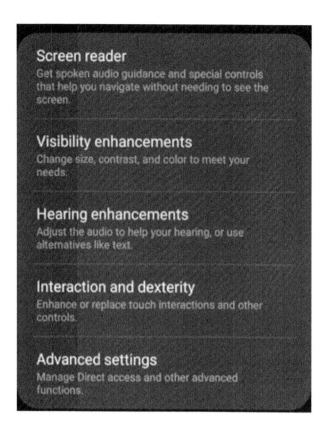

Let's dig in a little more what you will find in each of the menus.

SCREEN READER

Screen reader reads back whatever is on your phone. Push a button? It reads what that button says. Tapping the toggle will turn it on.

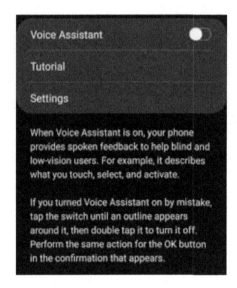

Clicking on settings will bring up settings for the voice. You can change how fast it speaks, if it speaks passwords and caller ID aloud, and more.

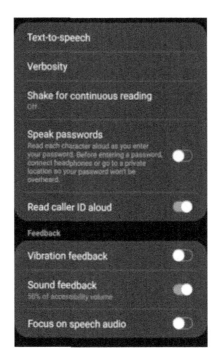

Visibility Enhancements

Visibility Enhancements changes the contrasts for people who have difficulty seeing. It also lets you change the shapes of buttons to make them stand out more.

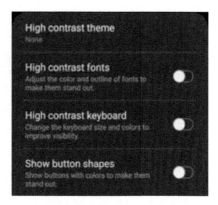

Under Size and Zoom you can turn magnification on and off; this is useful if you want apps to be larger, so you can read things without glasses.

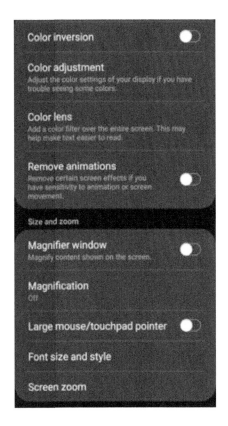

Hearing Enhancements

Hearing enhancements is where you go to make things amplified, change to mono audio, and add hearing aid support. You can also turn on Real Time Text and Live Captioning so you can read what you might not otherwise be able to hear.

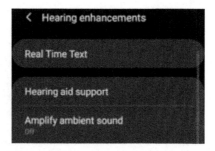

At the bottom of settings is Sound detectors, which lets you get notifications on your phone when it detects that someone has rang your doorbell or there's a baby crying.

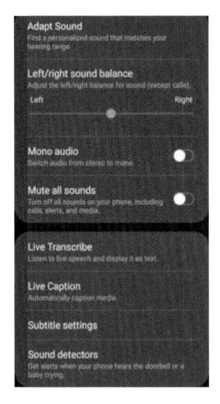

INTERACTION AND DEXTERITY

If you find that when you tap, things don't open, then Interaction and Dexterity is a setting that can help adjust the sensitivity of touch, which may make it more responsive.

212 | Google Searching Like a Pro

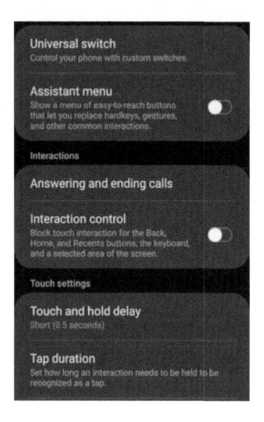

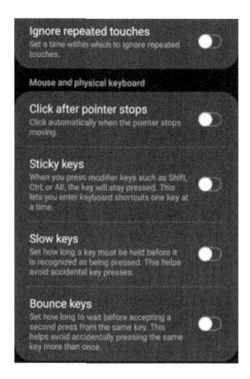

ADVANCED SETTINGS

The advance menu lets you turn your volume up / down and side button into shortcut keys. For example, you can set volume up to open an app instead of turn the volume up. You can also set up flash notifications, so your flash goes off anytime that you get an alert.

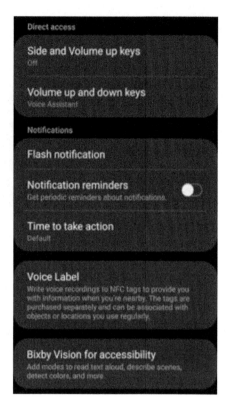

SOFTWARE UPDATE

This is where you will find general information about your phone, such as the OS you are running, the kind of phone you have, IP address, etc. It's more of an FYI, but there are a few settings here that you can change.

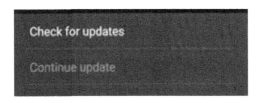

TIPS & SUPPORT

This isn't really a setting. It's just tips and support. You can also talk with support here.

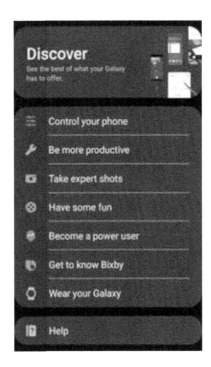

ABOUT PHONE

This is where you will find general information about your phone. Such as the OS you are running, the kind of phone you have, IP address, etc. It's more of an FYI, but there are a few settings here that you can change.

[8]

ADD-ONS

This chapter will cover:
- Project Fi
- Galaxy accessories
- Third-party accessories

PROJECT FI?

In 2015, Google launched something they called Project Fi. It's their vision of what a cell phone network is supposed to be. A shared plan with a healthy amount of data. You pay for what you need—not what the provider tells you. It's sort of a hybrid of using data and using wi-fi to get you good speeds for a price that's quite a bit cheaper than others.

How much cheaper? It depends, but my guess is cheaper than what you are paying.

As of this writing, it starts at $20. That gets you unlimited minutes and text. But no data. Let's say you are a very light data user and only needed 1GB. It would cost you a total of $30—taxes and fees included. If you are a data hog and stream everything you can 24/7, then you would want the top plan, 20 GB. That would cost you $80. Total. What if you go over 20GB? Same price! Your speed is slowed—that's the catch. It's guaranteed fast until 20GB, however. According to Google, less than 1% of all people use more than 15GB...so chances are, you'll be fine.

What about families? For a family of six, the most you would pay is $275—that's, again, sharing 20GB. You can see a calculator at https://fi.google.com/about/plan/.

S PEN

The S Pen used to be exclusive to the Galaxy Note; that changed in 2021, when it was introduced to the Ultra series. It's built into the S22 Ultra, but sold separately with other phones. It retails for $39.99, but you can frequently find it cheaper bundled with either the phone or phone case.

The pen is very simple, yet powerful to use. Tap the screen to activate it. When it's activated, you'll see a small icon on your screen with controls (known as the Air Command).

When you tap that icon, you'll see all kinds of shortcuts available

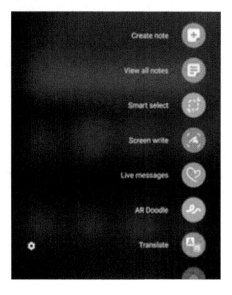

You can also tap the config button to show an expanded list of S Pen settings. This includes shortcut actions.

< S Pen

On

Screen off memo

Create note with Pen button

Air view
On

Show pointer when hovering

Air command

Shortcuts

Show floating icon

Open Air command with Pen

Bonus Book: Google Search Pro Tips

This chapter will cover:
- What is a Boolean search?
- Google Search Operators
- Basic commands

THE MATH OF SEARCHING

History lesson time: becoming a Google search expert owes a lot of credit to math. If you are like me—someone who needs a calculator for simple addition—then you are probably thinking, "Oh, no! Time to close this book and forget I ever thought about becoming better at Google search!"

Don't worry! You'll be fine! It owes a lot to math, but it doesn't look like the kind of math that you ran from in high school.

The math we are talking about is Boolean algebra. Basically, it's the kind of problems with true / false statements.

When you are using Boolean in traditional math it can get a little complicated; in a search, not so much. A typical Boolean search is going to look a little like this:

Boolean AND search

What's the purpose of this kind of search? Precision. It makes it easier to find what you want without combing through lots of webpages.

There are three main types of Boolean searches: AND, NOT, and OR.

You probably already guessed what they do. AND searches both terms, which Google already does.

NOT excludes terms. For example, let's say you want to search for administrator jobs that aren't related to being a manager. You could search for:

Administrator NOT manager

OR searches for either or. For example:

Computer OR pc

Not exactly the math you are used to, right?

GOOGLE SEARCH OPERATORS

Google has a whole set of commands that go beyond the typical Boolean ones above (which you can also use). They call these Google Search Operators.

There are dozens of "operators"—Google frequently adds more (and takes away others); so, if something in this book doesn't work, make sure you have read it right, but remember there is a chance that Google took it out.

As an example, a few years back, you could use this to find phone numbers:

Phonebook:john doe

This is no longer the case.

One search operator that's been around for years is the calculator. Google "calculator" and you'll see a working calculator appear in your search. That's pretty cool, right? What's cooler is you can just search for equations.

For example, I'll type in 60*8 (the * means times—FYI, the divide sign looks like this /):

You can make your calculations pretty complex; for example, here's what (60*8)/(12)+8 looks like:

Google's search calculator can do more than basic math. You can search for conversions, too. It's helpful for cooking and pretty much everything else.

Here's how it would look if you wanted to know what 100 feet is in inches:

Remember: this stuff works on the mobile version of search as well. So, let's say you are travelling and need to know how much something is in USD—just search for it. Here's an example of a search for 200 yen to usd:

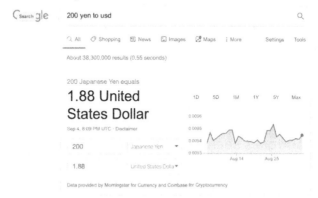

COMMON GOOGLE SEARCH OPERA-TORS

As I've already mentioned, there are dozens of operators, but this section will cover the most common you will use.

Price

If you are hunting for a product, then search for it with a price value. For example, let's say you want a Chromebook, and your budget is $200. Search "Chromebook $200" and you'll get results like this:

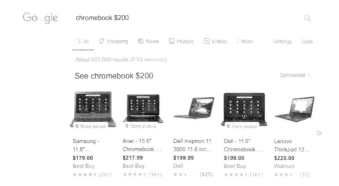

The above search will give you a pretty broad range of computers. If you know your budget, then you can search for that as well. Let's say your budget is $200 to $250 for that Chromebook. That search would look like this:

Chromebook $200...$250

Exclude Words

Sometimes you search for things that have more than one meaning. As an example, think about the word "Bronco." There's the Ford Bronco truck, but also a horse named the bronco and a football team. What if you want to know the speed of a bronco, but you are referring to the horse, not the truck? Use the minus (-) key:

Bronco speed -truck

Exact Matches

When you search for words in Google, it's looking for the term—but also looking for pages that have each of the words. If you only want to find the exact term, then you can add quotes. For example, instead of searching broadly for:

Tallest man

You can use quotes: "Tallest man." In the first example, it's looking for webpages that contain both tallest and man in any combination. In the second, it's only looking for that exact phrase.

You can also combine search with the Boolean searches above (e.g. AND, OR, NOT). For example:

"Tallest man" AND "United States"

Excluding Words and Wildcards

If there are words you absolutely do not want, then you can use the minus (-) key. If there's a term you want either, but not necessarily both, of the words (for example it can be a webpage with Disneyland or Theme park) then you can do a wildcard search with the * key (e.g. "Disneyland * Theme park").

Site Search

Google can do more than search millions of pages—it also can search just one page. What I mean by that is you can do a Google search on a specific domain. Just put "Site:" in your search and the domain you are searching for. For example, let's say I wanted to find out about the literature programs at Cal State Fullerton University. I can use this search term to do that:

Site:Fullerton.edu literature

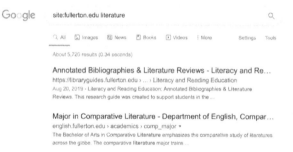

Related Search

Have you ever read a news website or visited an ecommerce store and wanted to see similar websites? Related search lets you do that. Simply add "Related:" and the domain you want to see similar websites to into your search bar. For example, if I wanted to see websites that are similar to Amazon.com, I would Google this:

Related:amazon.com

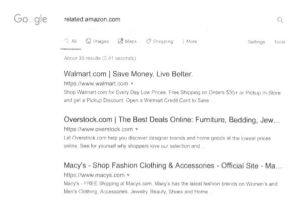

MORE GOOGLE SEARCH OPERATORS

The next operators are useful, but not as commonly used.

Around Search

Some of these searches get a little complicated. An around search is one such search. The search looks for terms close together. Let's say you are looking up a politician's stance on immigration. You want to search for the politician's name mentioned around the word immigration, specifying how many words should separate them. For example, if I want to find "Biden" within six words of "immigration," I would search for this:

Biden AROUND(6) immigration

That tells Google to make sure the two terms are only six words apart or less. If "Biden" appears in the first paragraph, and "immigration" appears several paragraphs down, then it wouldn't come up as a result.

Definitions

Is there a word you don't know and want the definition? Don't go to your dictionary! Just Google "Define:" and you'll get the definition at the top of your results. Such as:

Define: onomatopoeia

Cache
A cache search is something commonly used for marketers doing SEO reviews, but not so much for everyday searchers. It shows you the page that Google has most recently crawled (which means the last time a bot went to the page to see if it had been updated). To perform the search just type in "Cache:" and the website. For example (make sure you don't leave a space):

Cache:whitehouse.gov

Filetype
If you are looking for a document—not a website—a file search will help you out. Let's say it's tax season and you need your 1099. You don't want to go to the instructional website that tells you about the form. You just want the form. Try this search:

1099 filetype:PDF

Notice how all the results have a PDF in them?

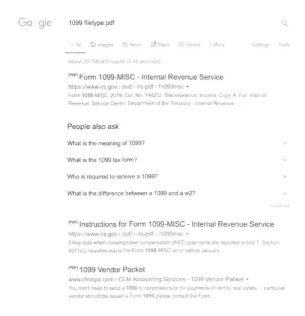

This also works for other file types (DOCX, TXT, PPT, and more—if you don't see the filetype there, then experiment because it may have been added by the time of this writing).

Group Items

If you have multiple terms you want to group together, then you can use "( )". For example, let's say you are interested in two products from the same company; you could use a term like this:

(switch OR 3ds) Nintendo

Map

If you want a map of a city, just search for "Map:" and the name of the city. For example:

Map: Anaheim

If you need a map of a specific address, just type in the address (no need to add "map" to the search). You'll get a zoomed-in view (sometimes it will have a street view as well), and in the lower right corner, there's an option for directions.

Movie Showtimes

Heading to the movies? Google "Movie:" and the name of the movie to get the latest showtimes. For example:

Movie: Spider Man Far From Home

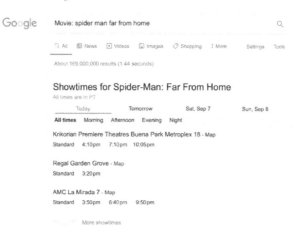

Notice how it doesn't ask for locations? That's because it knows my location based on my IP. That's kind of convenient, but what if I'm going to another location to see the movie? Just add a location to the end. For example:

Movie: Spider Man Far From Home New York City

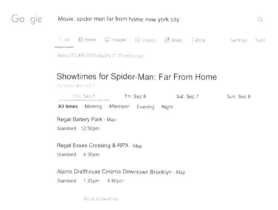

Source Search

Later in this book, I'll talk about different places to search (image search, news search, video search, etc). This search query applies to news search, which you can perform at google.com/news. If you want to see only a specific newspaper, magazine, or blog, then search "Source:" and the name of the publication. For example:

Source: New York Times

Stock Search

If you are a financial buff, you can search for ticker information (such as current price) by typing "Stock:" and the ticker symbol (some companies will still come up if you type the company name and not the symbol, but the symbol is always the best practice). For example:

Stock:dis

You also have the option to follow the stock by clicking on the blue button in the upper right corner.

Title Search

Something that's helpful when looking for news articles is an Intitle search. It finds websites, too. What the search does is looks for the term in the page title. For example:

Intitle:Microsoft

You can search for multiple terms in the title with "Allintitle" For example:

Allintitle:Microsoft surface

You can also search for terms in the text (not title) with "Intext" and "Allintext."

URL Search

Very similar to the Intitle search is the Inurl search. Where the Intitle search searches the page title, the Inurl searches URLs. So, if you are looking for websites that have Paleo in the URL, then search for this:

Inurl:paleo

Just as you can search for all terms with "Allintitle," you can search for all terms in URL with "Allinurl." For example:

Allinurl:paleo recipes

Weather

Forget the weather apps or going to webpages for the weather, just type in "Weather:" and the city to your search and get the forecast in your results. For example:

Weather:Kabul

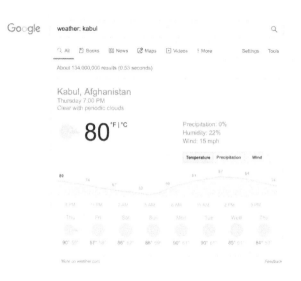

ADVANCED GOOGLE SEARCH SETTINGS

Did you know that Google keeps track of what you are searching for? Anyone who shares a computer with you can go in and see your search history if you are still signed in.

It's not a problem for me. I could care less if anyone in my house sees I've searched way too many times for what time *Full House* is on TV! It does become a problem during the Christmas search when people in my house like to see what presents I've been searching for! So, knowing how to delete it is helpful.

When you do a basic Google search, there's two options at the end that many people don't notice or use. Settings and Tools. Tools lets you filter your results.

Settings is where you can see some of the more advanced settings. When you click it, a drop down appears.

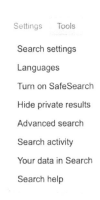

One option is to "Hid private results" which is helpful if you know you don't want your search saved.

To see your search history, go to Search Activity.

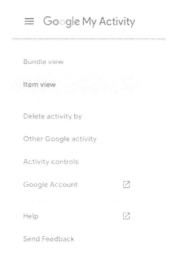

In addition to viewing your activity, you can click "Delete activity by" to delete your saved search. You can delete by dates too.

If you head over to Search Settings you will also be able to configure things like how many search results appear on a page.

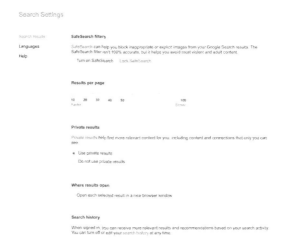

Just remember when you change anything to go to the bottom and save your results.

[2]

SEARCHING BEYOND WEBPAGES

This chapter will cover:
- Searching for books
- Searching for finance
- Searching for flights
- Searching for images
- Searching for maps
- Searching for news
- Searching for products
- Searching for videos
- Searching for you!

BEYOND GOOGLING

If you've ever "Google'd" something, then you probably started with google.com. That's a great place to start...for some keywords. But Google has evolved over the years and created more than just a web search engine.

If you are searching for images, for example, then you can use an entirely different search engine.

The operators I showed you in the first chapter will largely apply to these searches as well—it's a bit hit or miss, so some will work better than others.

Some are more complicated than others. I'll cover each one here. As with all things in this book, remember that Google takes things out and adds things in regularly, so if you don't see it, then chances are they've removed it.

You can see all the different types of searches you can perform when you do a regular Google search. Notice all the options below the search? Including one that says more?

SEARCHING FOR BOOKS

The first option I'll cover is books. You can find it here:

Google.com/books

As you might have guessed, it searches for books. At first glance, it looks pretty simple. It's just a search bar. (If you've downloaded books from the Google Play store, those will show up on a bookshelf below that.)

You may be thinking, "Nice…but I find my books at Amazon or Barnes & Noble."

I don't blame you for thinking that. Those are both great places to buy books. Google, however, is a great place to find books, too. Why? Because the filters are more advanced. They've also worked with a lot of universities to digitalize collections, so you can find electronic copies of books and search inside them—sometimes they're even free. A lot of these books are rare and out of print.

On the right corner of the search, there's a config button. When you click on that, there's an option for "Advanced Book Search."

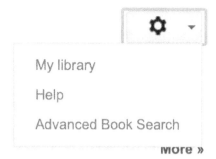

The advanced search gives you over a dozen options to narrow your search.

For this book, I'll do a very basic search for "Hurricanes."

Once the results come back, I can start filtering them. I can show, for example, all books, or only books with previews, or only books that are free.

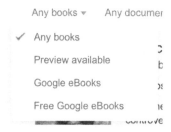

Next to "Any books" I can search for the type of document I'm looking for (e.g. any, books, magazines, newspapers).

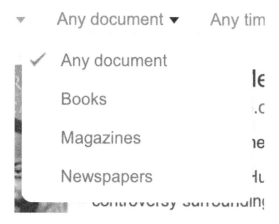

Finally, I can search for when it was published. This is especially useful if you have a specific range or are looking for a rare book—for example, you want to read what people were saying about the flu in 1751.

▼ Any time ▼   Sorted by

✓ Any time

r

ɔ   21st century

,   20th century

n   19th century   ⲧ

ˑy   ⲓr

ˮ€   Custom range...   ꜱ

SEARCHING FOR FINANCE

The finance search is a bit like having a financial newspaper in the cloud—except you make it more personal. To get to it, go to:

Google.com/finance

The first thing you'll see is a dashboard with all the markets—and, if you follow any, companies you follow.

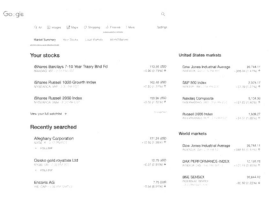

If you scroll down on the page, you'll see local market news.

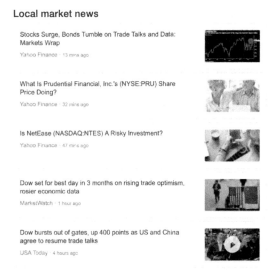

And further down, world market news.

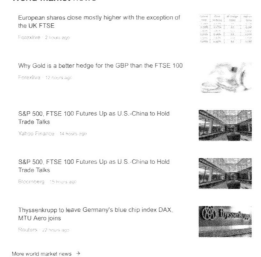

World market news

European shares close mostly higher with the exception of the UK FTSE
Forexlive · 2 hours ago

Why Gold is a better hedge for the GBP than the FTSE 100
Forexlive · 12 hours ago

S&P 500, FTSE 100 Futures Up as U.S.-China to Hold Trade Talks
Yahoo Finance · 14 hours ago

S&P 500, FTSE 100 Futures Up as U.S.-China to Hold Trade Talks
Bloomberg · 15 hours ago

Thyssenkrupp to leave Germany's blue chip index DAX, MTU Aero joins
Reuters · 22 hours ago

More world market news →

Up top—right under the search box—there are four different options for different markets.

Market Summary   Your Stocks   Local Markets   World Markets

The search itself is pretty basic. You search for companies. Instead of a traditional search where you get webpages, however, it shows you the current state of the stock. There's also a follow button in blue if you want to add the company to your finance dashboard.

Below the stock information, you can get all the company news.

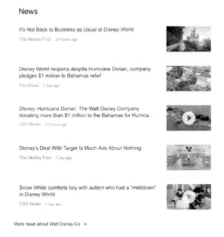

And below the news, you can grab the company's quarterly financial report.

Quarterly financials

(USD)	Jun 2019	Y/Y
Revenue	20.25B	32.94% ↑
Net income	1.76B	39.64% ↓
Diluted EPS	0.97	50.26% ↓
Net profit margin	8.69%	54.62% ↓

More financials →

SEARCHING FOR TRAVEL

Expedia, Priceline, and similar travel sites are great, but Google takes it up a notch with more filtering and integration with their own services (such as Google Maps). When you use their search, you are usually booking through the actual airline or hotel, with Google managing things on the backend. It's just as secure as any other travel website.

To check out how it works go to:

Google.com/flights

As the URL implies, flights are what the search is known for, and they are the first thing you see. But there's more here, as you'll quickly learn.

When you search for your trip, you can do all the standard filters you can do pretty much anywhere else—make it one way, add passengers, and switch from economy to business or first class.

Round trip ▼   1 passenger ▼   Economy ▼

As you search for the dates, you can also see about how much it will cost—this is helpful if your dates are flexible as it helps you find the cheapest time to travel.

After you search for the flight, you can begin filtering by price, how many stops, and more.

You can also track the price to see if it goes up or down over time.

If you want to see how much it is on different dates, those options are shown again; in addition, you can see how much the flight is at a nearby airport—sometimes rates are cheaper if you go to a smaller airport.

When you are ready to book, you'll have the option once more to pick the fare that you want—economy, first class, etc.

On the left side, there's a menu with several other options. Let's look at hotels next.

One of the first things you'll notice when you do a hotel search is there's an option to look for both hotels and vacation rentals.

To make sure you are getting what you want, you can filter by reviews.

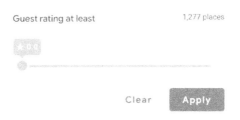

You can filter by the amenities they offer.

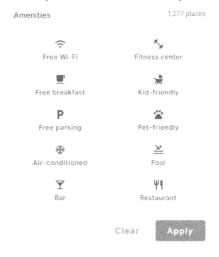

And you can search only for certain companies (e.g. Hilton, Marriot, etc).

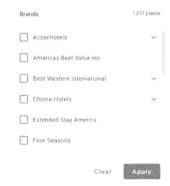

There are also options to filter by the hotel class.

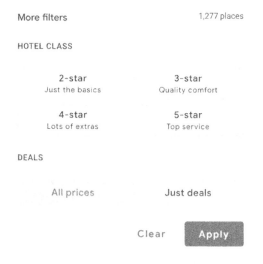

Finally, you have the option to filter by a specific price point / range.

The map on the right side shows you where different hotels are located, which is helpful if you will be seeing people nearby.

If you want to bundle your flight and hotel together—which usually gives you a slightly discounted rate—then click the "Packages" option on the left menu.

One of my favorite features about this Google search is the menu option labelled "Explore." This helps you see all the popular sites and attractions for the city.

If you click "Day plans" on the top, it will give you sample itineraries (note: this option is not available for all cities).

As an example, I clicked on "If you only have a day" and it gave me a list of what to see and a map of how to do it. Each step tells me how long it will take by car (subway is also available, depending on the city and where it's located in the city).

Right above the location, if I click how long it takes by car, it will take me to a map with driving directions.

Up on the top of this map is a list of all the different ways you can get there (subway, bike, walking, etc). Some will obviously be greyed out as you can't fly to the locations. The direction times will change based on what you pick—and, in the case of walking, it will take you down one-way streets.

SEARCHING FOR IMAGES

Google Images is a powerful tool if you are looking for images to stick into presentations, term papers, or anything else.

It's always important to remember that images can have copyrights, so make sure you understand the terms before using one publicly.

To get started with an image search, go here:

Google.com/images

It looks much like a normal Google search at first. Type in what you want a picture of and search away.

The biggest difference is the camera button next to the magnifying glass. Click that and you can search by an image's URL, or you can upload the image. Uploading an image is especially useful if you want to see if other people are using your work without your permission.

For this book, I'm going to search for puppies because who doesn't love puppies?

Some searches have smarter results than others. In this case, it tells me different breeds I can search for. You won't always see those suggestions.

Over in the upper right corner, there's a drop box that says, "Filter explicit results." Because this is an image search, this makes sure nothing inappropriate slips through. Use it or don't use it, but know that Google doesn't censor, so sometimes things come up that you may not expect to see.

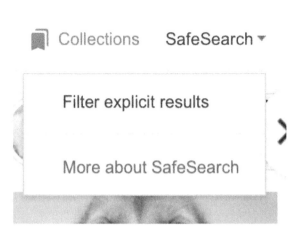

Near the right side, there's an option that says "Tools." When you click that, you'll see all the different filters.

The filters are largely self-explanatory. Size lets you show only photos that are a certain size—if you want a wallpaper for your computer, for example, you would select large.

Color lets you look for full color, black and white, transparent, or a certain shade. Transparent means the background is clear, FYI.

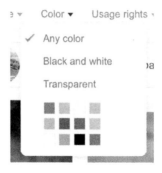

Usage rights can help you find photos you can reuse without permission. Be careful here! Just because it says it's fine, doesn't necessarily mean it is. It could be misclassified, someone else could have put it up without the person's permission, or a number of other things. If you are using a photo you found on a Google Image search commercially, then do so at your own risk.

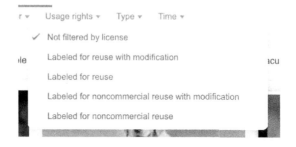

Type lets you pick the file type—if you are searching for an animated GIF for an email, for example.

Time is when the photo was added.

When you click the image, you get a preview on the right side.

You also have the option to share or bookmark it.

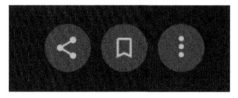

If you click on the image, it opens to the webpage containing the image.

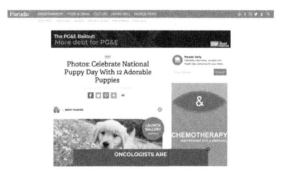

If you only want to open the image, then go back to your results, right click the image, and click "Open image in new tab."

That opens the page with only the image.

From It's a Puppy's Life by Seth Casteel

SEARCHING FOR MAPS

Google Maps is probably something you've used before. It comes up whenever you do normal searches for restaurants and businesses. But you can also search there directly here:

Google.com/maps

The common story you should notice by now is it's a very simple user interface.

The top left corner is where you do your searching. Before you search, however, you can also browse. So, for example, let's say you are looking for something to eat in your area. Just click the restaurant button.

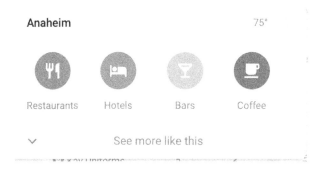

If you don't see what you want, click "See more like this" and then select the grey "More" button, which brings down several other options.

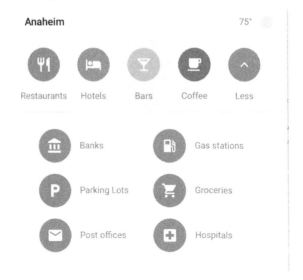

Once you click what you want (I'm using "Restaurants" in this example) you'll get a list of the results with reviews. Clicking on any of them will show you where it's at on the map; it will also show you the hours, website (if available), photos, and more.

When you click "Restaurants," you can also go back to that search and click at the end of the word. This will bring up an autocomplete that asks you if you want to see only nearby restaurants.

You can filter your results by price, ratings, hours, and type of cuisine.

On the lower right side, you can use the little yellow man to get a street view of your location.

Drag him wherever you want to see on the map.

That will bring up a street view of the location.

SEARCHING FOR NEWS

If you are a news junky and want to search for news stories, head over to:

Google.com/news

While the news search is pretty cool, it's not the research tool you are hoping for if you are serious about finding information. Many sources here will show you the current news, but make you pay for older news. If you need to find older stories, visit your local library—most libraries subscribe to news databases that are free to use; many of these can be used at home if you have a library card from that library.

The news section on the left side lets you sort your news by subject.

Top stories

For you

Favorites

Saved searches

U.S.

World

Local stories

Business

Technology

Entertainment

Sports

Science

Health

Language & region
English (United States)

Settings

When you search for news, you can click the little arrow on the right side of the search bar to bring down a more advanced search. Here you can search for phrases and dates.

SEARCHING FOR PRODUCTS

Google isn't exactly known for shopping, but it's definitely worth checking out. You can see it here:

Google.com/shopping

You can either search or browse for products.

When you search for products, there are a lot of filters on the left menu that you can apply.

One of the more helpful ones is "available nearby" which helps you find stores in the area that sell the product.

Show only

Buy with Google

Available nearby

New items

You can also shop by price point.

Price

Up to $250   ◯
$250 – $500   ◯
Over $500   ◯

$ _____ to

$ _____

GO

Depending on what you are searching for, there will be several unique filters. In the example below I searched "iPhone," and Google then let me filter by things like battery life.

Battery Life

10 – 14 hours   ◯

14 – 21 hours   ◯

Over 21 hours   ◯

By default, you'll get your results in a list, but clicking on the grid button in the right corner switches the layout.

In the upper left corner is the button to bring up settings.

This lets you see your orders, saved searches, and more.

SEARCHING FOR VIDEOS

Google owns YouTube and it makes sense that you would search for videos there. Using the search engine at the below link, however, will search for videos on YouTube and beyond:

Google.com/videohp

The search looks almost identical to the main Google search.

The results page, however, is a little bit different.

When you click tools on the right side (below the magnifying glass) you'll get expanded filters that you can apply (it's very similar to how image searching works).

You can search by duration, which is helpful if you are looking for a full movie and not just a clip.

When it was uploaded.

Any time ▾   Any quali

✓ Any time

Past hour

Past 24 hours

Past week

Past month

Past year

Custom range...

If you want it in any quality or if it has to be HD.

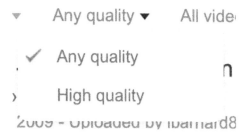

▾   Any quality ▾   All vide

✓ Any quality

〉   High quality

If you only want videos with closed captioning.

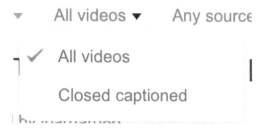

▾   All videos ▾   Any source

✓ All videos

Closed captioned

And finally, if you want to see a specific source that the video is coming from.

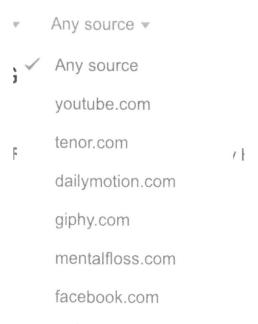

Many of the matches in the results also let you see similar videos. Look for the drop-down arrow next to the link if it applies.

SEARCHING FOR YOU!

The Google Personal Search is something Google has added and dropped and added again—so there's a chance it could be dropped again in the future.

A Google Personal Search looks through your personal files for matches—things like email and photos. It's all private, so even though it kind of looks like a Google search results page, nobody but you can see it.

Unlike other searches that have a dedicated domain, the easiest place to start a personal search is at google.com. Just type in what you are looking for.

When the results come back, click the "More" button and select "Personal."

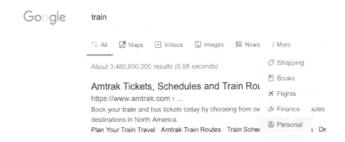

You can use the Google Personal Search to find photos.

Your photos
Only you can see these results

Emails.

Gmail
Only you can see these results

And the websites you have been browsing.

Your browsing history
Only you can see these results

[3]

GOOGLE ALERTS

This chapter will cover:
- What are alerts?
- How to create alerts
- How to delete alerts

DID SOMEONE JUST TALK ABOUT ME ONLINE?!

Admit it: you've "Google'd" yourself! It's okay! We all have. Call it the narcissist inside us, but we want to know what people are saying about us.

And chances are, they weren't saying a lot—unless your name happens to start with Brad and end with Pitt. If that's the case, then thanks for reading—would you like to read the screenplay I'm working on, Mr. Pitt?

Google Alert is a handy tool to get notified whenever someone talks about you or something you are interested in.

What happens is anytime Google crawls a web result with the term you want, it will email you. You can set it up as a digest (so you get all the results once a week, for example) or as it happens.

A word of caution: this is a tool for less common searches. You don't want to add an alert for something like "election" because there are thousands of pages with that term that get added every day.

It's better for less-used terms—such as some indie author you read who wouldn't be in the news very often.

CREATING AN ALERT

To create an alert, go to google.com/alerts in your browser (make sure you are signed into your Google account—if you are not, it will prompt you to login or create a free account).

Near the bottom, it will give you a few suggestions for alerts. It will suggest at the top that you
create an alert for your name or email.

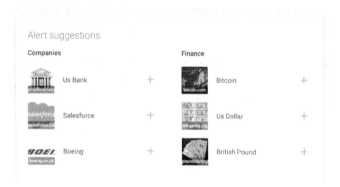

For this example, I'm going to create an alert
for the author, John Grisham—not exactly an indie
author, but I'm using this example to show how
you can put limits on the results, so your inbox isn't
flooded with news.

As soon as you type it in—before you even create the alert—you'll get a preview of the types of
news you'll see with this keyword.

Once you click the blue "Create Alert" button, you'll see the option to apply filters. If you are doing a popular term, I would suggest you change "How often" to make sure you don't get the news as it happens.

Sources lets you pick where the news is coming from. For example, if you only want alerts from news searches, or when the name is mentioned in a book.

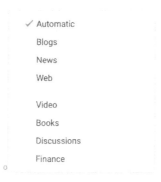

EDITING AND DELETING AN ALERT

Once you have added an alert, it will show up in your feed.

There are a few new options next to the alert. First, the pencil:

This brings back the previous menu where you can change how often it comes, the source, etc.

The next option is the config button:

This lets you update when you receive the alert and whether it's a digest or single email. Make sure to save your choice if you select something.

☐ **Delivery time**
Choose when to receive your alerts.

☐ **Digest**
Receive all alerts in a single email.

CANCEL   SAVE

The last option is the trashcan:

As you might expect, this lets you delete an alert. Once you delete it, you'll get a confirmation message:

Your alert on John Grisham has been deleted. Undo Dismiss

INDEX

Printed in Great Britain
by Amazon

26625711R00169

ABOUT THE AUTHOR

Scott La Counte is a UX Designer and writer. His first book, *Quiet, Please: Dispatches from a Public Librarian* (Da Capo 2008) was the editor's choice for the Chicago Tribune and a Discovery title for the Los Angeles Times.

He has written dozens of best-selling how-to guides on tech products.

He teaches UX Design at UC Berkeley.

You can connect with him at ScottDouglas.org.